Discover Educational Toys For Children

2ND EDITION

Discover Educational Toys For Children

2ND EDITION

Hilary Werdel

Edited by
Tracy Watkins

Scholar Books
San Francisco

Published by Scholar Books
P.O. Box 471048
San Francisco, CA 94147
email: SCHOLARBOOKS@hotmail.com
Call toll-free to order: 800-444-2524
Distributed by BookWorld Services, Inc.

ISBN 0-9655329-1-7

Printed in the United States of America
on recycled paper.

Acknowledgements

I extend my gratitude to all of the organizations, companies, and museums that responded to my request for information so enthusiastically. I am also grateful for my friends and family who encouraged and helped me along the way. I would especially like to thank Tracy Watkins for her work as editor and Kelly Dickerson for her advice as an educator.

A hundred years from now it is not going to matter what kind of car we drove or possessions we had – what matters is that we touch the life of a child that can change the course of the world.

–Unknown

Table of Contents

WEB SITES

Introduction:

Hilary Werdel is an industrial product designer and researches children's products and organizations. She holds a degree in Design from the University of California Los Angeles and studied industrial design at the Art Center College of Design. After using educational products in school to research electronics she felt that more children should benefit from these wonderful products. Finding no available resource of strictly educational products and organizations, she decided to write her own with the goal to provide a fun and educational resource for parents and educators alike.

Letter to the readers:

In my research, I have read hundreds of reports and have selected the products and catalogs which received favorable reviews or awards. I have also included products that are hard to find but provide valuable information.

This book is meant to provide a reference guide to educational products for children and teenagers. You may live in a town with limited resources to buy products for children or you may have limited time to spend shopping. All of the products listed can either be purchased through a catalog or over the internet and many can be shipped internationally.

I have included the section on museums because
they are a wonderful way to get children actively
involved in learning. They are such a great resource
and have so much to offer. Many people go to their
local museum for an occasional visit and do not know
about all the workshops or demonstrations it may
offer. This is also something to take advantage of
when you are traveling with your family. You may
want to call to see if the museum is offering any
workshops or if there will be a demonstration given
at a particular time while you are visiting the area.
Educators can also use museums as a source for
materials such as movies, specimens and publications
that can be checked out on loan.

There are thousands of sites on the web. I have
included only the sites that I feel have information
related to the education or welfare of children. All of
the sites have either been awarded with honors or
have received a positive review. It has been my inten-
tion to only include web sites that do not contain
violent or inappropriate material for school children
but unfortunately because of the rate at which things
change on the internet, I can not guarantee that all
of the material is safe for young children.
If you have difficulty finding a web site, check to
make sure you have entered the correct http or
gopher address. The next step is to go to a search
engine such as www.yahoo.com and enter the title of
the web site then press search to find the new web
address.

There are many resources for information on software and computers for families. A few more excellent sources are Newsweek Computers & the Family and Family PC. For comparative pricing on computer hardware, software and furniture go to the web site Pricewatch at http://www.pricewatch.com.

For advice on safely purchasing products online visit the web site from the Consumer Information Center and the Federal Trade Commission called Cybershopping: Protecting Yourself Online. The internet address is http://www.ftc.gov/bcp/conline/pubs/buying/cybersho.htm. If you experience fraud on the internet, report it to the National Fraud Information Center. Their phone number is 800-876-7060 and their web site address is http://www.fraud.org. Carefully read all of the guarantees and return policies to ensure that the product you purchase may be returned if you are not satisfied.

I hope that you find this guide valuable and enjoyable. Your comments and suggestions are always welcome.

Hilary Werdel

Pricing

This book includes products ranging from less than $10 to $100+. Below is a sample of items typical to this guide:

Wood Blocks: An 82 piece set with 12 different shapes measuring 1 1/4" x 2 3/4" x 5 1/2" ranges from $114.95 to $179.00 with the best deal being the Supersaver block set from Constructive Playthings at $114.95.

Language Tools: All products in this section offer a wide variety of options and vary greatly in price, from Transparent Languages CD-ROM series called Language Now for $129.00 to Berlitz books and tapes for $15.00 to a Teacher Reproducible book by Twin Sisters Productions available for $6.99.

Magazines and Newspapers: Periodicals are a wonderful option as they continue to offer new information year around. The subscriptions suggested range from $8.50 for Career World to $46.00 for Biography Today which offers insight and inspiration that is well worth the value.

Software: The average price range for the software selected for this guide is $30 to $45 with the exception of the CD-ROMs from Kidsoft which are priced at $12.99.

PRODUCTS AND CATALOGS

CATALOGS SPECIALIZING IN CHILDHOOD

This chapter includes catalogs and products for children and teens. It is divided into sections each with their own heading. The first division includes catalogs that offer products that cover a range of interests such as science, math and literature. The following sections include catalogs that specialize in a particular product or area of interest such as music or safety.

Animal Town

Post Office Box 485
Healdsburg, California 95448
800-445-8642
Fax 707-837-9737

Animal Town has been in business for 20 years and produces an annual catalog of toys and games for **ages 6 months to adults**. They have a wonderful selection of unique board games and books.

Back To Basic Toys

31333 Agoura Road
Westlake Village, California 91361-4639
800-356-5360
Fax 818-865-8301
For International Orders 818-865-8301

Back To Basic Toys catalog carries products for **infants to age 13**. Their choices range from chalkboard easels to balance beams with a large selection of musical instruments including a child's size violin.

Builder Books, Inc.

Post Office Box 99
Riverside, Washington 98849
800-260-5461
509-826-6021
Fax 509-826-5624

> Builder Books is a discount catalog of educational materials for **all ages**. The subjects represented are early childhood, language arts, Bible based study, grammar and composition, spelling, vocabulary, foreign languages, handwriting, critical thinking, math games, science, biographies, history, economics, business, geography, cultures, music and art.

Constructive Playthings

1227 East 119th Street
Grandview, Missouri 64030-1117
800-832-0572

> Constructive Playthings is a catalog of products for **infants to age 10**. They have a wonderful selection of arts and crafts and inspiring books such as *The Children's Book of Virtues* edited by William J. Bennett.

Discovery Toys

2530 Arnold Drive
Martinez, California 94553
800-426-4777

> The Explorer Express product for **ages 2 to 5** was recognized as one of Dr. Toy's Top Children's

PRODUCTS AND CATALOGS
CATALOGS SPECIALIZING IN CHILDHOOD

Products. Call for a full color catalog of products for children of **all ages**.

Dorling Kindersley, Inc.

95 Madison Avenue
New York, New York 10016
800-356-6575
http://www.dk.com

> Dorling Kindersley, Inc. publishes The Ultimate Visual Dictionary for **ages 9 and up**. This reference guide uses annotated photographs and illustrations to define everything in our world from the universe to music. It is available in most large book stores or visit their web site for an online catalog.

Educational Insights

16941 Keegan Avenue.
Carson, California 90746
800-933-3277

> The Educational Insights **preK through 8th grade** catalog features science kits, archaeological sets, anatomy models, nature labs in addition to its variety of GeoSafari and MathSafari games and lessons.

Essential Learning Products

2300 West Fifth Avenue
Post Office Box 2590
Columbus, Ohio 43216-2590
614-486-0633
Fax 614-487-2272

Essential Learning Products has a selection of practice and activity books that focus on spelling, grammar, vocabulary, reading and math. This catalog for **kindergarten through 8th grade** also carries a variety of tools to improve handwriting skills.

FAO Schwarz

767 Fifth Avenue
New York, New York 10153
800-426-8097
http://faoschwarz.com

FAO Schwarz is famous for their large selection of deluxe toys for **all ages**. Their reputation is well deserved with unique and special offerings such as Ivan the Talking Chess Computer and the Astronomical Telescope.

Hand in Hand

Catalog Center
891 Main Street
Oxford, Maine 04270
800-872-9745

Hand in Hand is a catalog of children's products for **infants to age 10**. They carry many educational

toys, potty training tools, videos like See How They
Grow and books like Montessori Play and Learn.

HearthSong

Processing Center (address for mail orders only)
6519 N. Galena Road
Post Office Box 1773
Peoria, Illinois 61656-1773
800-325-2502
For the Hearing Impaired 800-228-2589
Fax 309-689-3857

HearthSong celebrates the seasons by selecting
products that reflect the time of the year. The catalog for **infants and children up to age 13** also has
a great selection of kits that involve crafts and activities.

Klutz Press

2121 Staunton Court
Palo Alto, CA 94306
800-558-8944
415-424-0739
http://www.klutz.com

The Klutz Catalogue and store offers many affordably
priced specialty products and activity books for children. Geared for **ages 6 to adult**, this catalog offers
educational books filled with information and humor
including products like the Time Book which makes
learning to tell time fun and comes with its own
watch. If you are planning to be in the area, call for a
calendar of events. They offer free classes on activi-

ties such as juggling that are usually 45 minutes to 1 hour long. Their store is located at 572 College Avenue, Palo Alto, California 94306. 415-493-2481.

The Learning Edge

4813 East Marshall Drive
Vestal, New York 13850
888-205-3276
607-722-6563

The learning edge is a catalog that includes many educational toys and games for **children and teens**. They have over 50 subject categories a few of which are Bible, foreign languages, physical education, physics and American history. Most of the products are offered at discounted prices.

Learning Resources

675 Heathrow Drive
Lincolnshire, Illinois 60069
800-222-3909
847-793-4500
Fax 800-222-0249

Learning Resources catalog carries products for children in **preK to 8th grade**. They feature a large selection of early math and language toys along with several science kits covering subjects such as electricity, ecology, simple machines, weather, light and sound.

Lego

555 Taylor Road
Post Office Box 1310
Enfield, Connecticut 06083-1310
800-453-4652
Fax 860-763-6800

> The Lego World of Adventures catalog is filled with over 200 fascinating lego sets for children **ages 8 to 12** to build.

Library Video Company

Post Office Box 1110
Bala Cynwyd, Pennsylvania 19004
800-843-3620
Fax 610-667-3425

> If you are looking for an educational video, this is the catalog to have. You will discover videos for **all ages** focusing on cultures, history, authors, black studies, business, children's stories, classic literature, computing, cooking, education, exercise and health, foreign languages, geography, music and dance, mythology and legends, nature, parenting, science and sports.

PlayFair Toys

Post Office Box 18210
Boulder, Colorado 80308
800-824-7255
Fax 303-440-3393

> PlayFair Toys is a catalog of toys and play equipment

for **toddlers to age 10**. They have a selection of outdoor play and sports equipment along with educational games.

Quality Education Resources

Post Office Box 847

Cupertino, California 95015-0847

408-252-2254

Fax 408-973-0470

Mathematics, science, social studies, english, logic, fine arts, parent resources and early childhood are just a few of the subjects covered in the Quality Education Resources catalog. They have entertaining books, kits and games for every subject such as Challenge Through American History, a trivia board game with over 1,440 questions.

School Zone Publishing

Post Office Box 777

Grand Haven, Michigan 49417

800-253-0564

Fax 616-846-6181

http://www.schoolzone.com

School Zone publishes activity books, workbooks, flash cards, puzzle cards, game cards, beginner reading books, software and more for **ages 3 to 10**. Their colorfully illustrated products involve shapes, colors, math, reading, mazes, dot-to-dot and more. Call for a catalog and ask for a parent order form.

Sensational Beginnings

Post Office Box 2009
987 Stewart Road
Monroe, Michigan 48162
800-444-2147

> Sensational Beginnings catalog carries a wide range of products such as the Teaching Clock and the Home Planetarium. They carry products appropriate for **infants to age 11**.

The Smithsonian Institution

Department 006, West D.C.
800-322-0344 USA
703-455-1700 Foreign Inquiries
Fax 703-455-4843
http://www.si.edu

> Although their educational products are not readily apparent, this catalog usually has 2 to 3 pages of quality educational toys for **children ages 2 to 12**. Such as floor puzzles and science kits. Call for a free catalog or visit their web site to pursue their products online.

Smithsonian Institution Press

Post Office Box 700
Holmes, Pennsylvania 19043-0700
800-863-9943 USA
703-455-1700 Foreign Inquiries
http://www.si.edu

> Call for a catalog of books, videos and discs covering history, space, artists, musicians and nature or visit

their web site. They have products for **children and adults**.

This Country's TOYS

Post Office Box 41479

Providence, Rhode Island 02940-1479

800-359-1233

Fax 800-359-6144

This Country's TOYS is a catalog that offers a wonderful selection of wooden blocks and wooden trains-on track with accessories for **ages 2 years and up**.

Toys To Grow On

Post Office Box 17

Long Beach, California 90801

800-542-8338

310-603-8890

Fax 310-537-5403

Toys To Grow On Catalog carries products for children **ages 2 to 13**. Their selection includes fun outdoor games as well as brain teasers like the Math Mysteries Problem Solving Box and the Self-Teaching Math Machines.

United Nations Children's Fund

Post Office Box 182233
Chattanooga, Tennessee 37422
800-553-1200
212-326-7000
Fax 212-888-7465

UNICEF publishes a perennial catalog of specialty products like games, books and puzzles suitable for children around the world **ages 1 and up**. Books such as Children Just Like Me offer a photographic introduction to several different cultures. While Games Around the World is published in English, French, Spanish and Portuguese and Lingo is a word game that teaches the names of food in eight languages. The United Nations Children Fund cooperates with governments in more than 140 countries to help provide clean water, health care, education and nutrition programs for children and mothers.

Ursa Major

Post Office Box 3368
Ashland, Oregon 97520
800-999-3433
Fax 503-482-5597

This brochure of stencil kits includes stencils of the night sky, the USA, the world map and a regulation basketball court. They also have an audio tape of night sounds to add to the excitement of the night sky.

ARTS AND HISTORY MATERIALS

Alcazar Music

Post Office Box 429, South Maine Street
Waterbury, Vermont 05676
800-541-9904
Fax 802-244-6128

> Alcazar Music is a catalog with a great selection of music and storytelling products designed specifically for **children of all ages**. Some of their classics include Louis Armstrong recorded Disney Songs The Satchmo Way, Alice In Wonderland, Where In The World Is Carmen Sandiego?, Noah and The Ark, Fun Phonics and a special holiday selection including everything from Christmas to Chanukah to Halloween. They also offer some great video series like Shakespeare; The Animated Tales, Richard Scary, School House Rock, Sesame Street and Thomas The Tank.

Anyone Can Whistle

323 Wall Street
Kingston, New York 12401
800-435-8863
Fax 914-339-3301
http:// www.anyonecan.com/acwhp.html

> Anyone Can Whistle is a catalog of easy-to-play instruments from around the world for children **ages 4 and up**. They also have a selection CDs and

wind chimes. Visit their web site for an online catalog.

Ars Nova

Box 637
Kirkland, Washington 98083-0637
800-445-4866
206-828-2711
Fax 206-889-0359
http://www.ars-nova.com

Ars Nova develops software for **all ages** designed to teach standard music notation as well as advanced music training in higher education. The title for children ages 3 to 13, A Little Kidmusic, provides a simple and logical way for children to learn music notation, pitch and rhythm. Older children can also write and record their own melodies. Practica Musica, a software title used in higher education, teaches beginning to advanced ear training and music theory. Songworks is a music notation program that allows you to experiment with harmony and melody or produce a leadsheet. All of the titles are for the Macintosh and MIDI compatible but MIDI is not required.

Audio Forum

96 Broad Street
Guilford, Connecticut 06437
800-243-1234
203-453-9794

Audio Forum has a wonderful selection of audio and

video programs celebrating music. They produce several catalogs so be sure to ask for the music catalog. Just a few of the topics covered are music history, learning to read music, masters of classical music, American Jazz, opera, ethnic music, dance, Leonard Bernstein's Young People's Concerts and music and songs for **children of all ages**.

The Concord Review

Post Office Box 661
Concord, Massachusetts 01742
800-331-5007
http://www.tcr.org

The Concord Review raises the standard for excellence in **high school** history classes. The quarterly journal publishes essays by students of history. The essays are challenging and impressive. They are a great way to teach and motivate students as well as bolster a college application by submitting an essay for publication.

The Discovery and Learning Channel

800-357-8800 Discovery and Learning Channel
800-938-0333 Discovery Channel Catalog
http://www.discovery.com

The Discovery and Learning Channel offers a positive alternative to regular programming by featuring educational shows on the arts, science, nature and much more. The Discovery Channel also has a product catalog including videos such as The Dead Sea Scrolls, The Last of the Czars, The Revolutionary War, Great

Palaces of the World and more.

Far Out Explorations

Post Office Box 308

Milford, Connecticut 06460

800-510-2787

203-877-2962

Far Out Explorations has a catalog of art books for **children of all ages** including adults. They have a selection of well priced books with titles such as Famous Children Composers, History of Art For Young People and the Museum of Modern Art series of books. Subjects covered range from architecture to dance.

Hands-On History

201 Constance Drive

New Lenox, Illinois 60451

Hands-On History is an American History Resource for enrichment materials, hands-on kits, historical books, videos, period toys and games. Send for more information by writing to the address above.

The History Channel

800-625-9000

The History Store has over 1,000 video titles covering biography, drama, documentary,performing arts and more. You can request a catalog or go to the website at http://www.historychannel.com.

Kimbo Educational

10 North Third Avenue
Post Office Box 477z
Long Branch, New Jersey 07740-0477
800-631-2187
Fax 908-870-3340
Outside the Continental U.S. 908-229-4949

Kimbo Educational is a catalog of educational musical products for infants and children **ages 3 to 15**. Musical lyrics are used to teach grammar, phonics, math, Spanish, French, German, Italian, Japanese, social skills and more. The majority of the CDs, cassettes and videos are accompanied by a guide. They also feature well priced nylon parachutes with handles and rhythmic parachute cassettes.

Kultur/ White Star Video

195 Highway 36
West Long Branch, New Jersey 07764-1409
800-458-5887
908-229-0066

This is a wonderful catalog of performing arts videocassettes featuring dance instruction, music instruction, children's titles, history and a variety of series covering opera, ballet, dance, music, jazz and the arts. For those just starting out they offer selections like, Fantasy Garden Ballet Class For Preschoolers, Tap Dancing for Beginners and Karate for Kids. They also have the Luciano Pavarotti Gala concert, Wagner: The Complete Epic, Sleeping Beauty, Magic of the Bolshoi Ballet, Carols for Christmas, Pavarotti at Julliard; Opera Master Class, Dizzy Gillespie; Live in London, Rembrandt, The Art of the Western World and Ancient Greece to entertain and intrigue **all ages**.

Miss Jackie Music Company

10001 El Monte
Overland Park, Kansas 66207-3631
800-432-6307
913-381-3672
Fax 913-381-8097

"Miss Jackie" Silberg has written a host of musical books, tapes, workshops and videos for infants to eight year olds. She holds degrees in Education and Child Development and her catalog includes titles such as Teaching Peace, Great Book of Rhythm, The Best of Early Childhood Music, Games To Play with Two Year Olds and Sing about Martin, a picture song depicting Dr. Martin Luther King's nonviolent struggle for civil rights.

Music for Little People

Post Office Box 1720
Lawndale, California 90260
800-727-2233
Fax 800-722-9505

This is a catalog of musical videos, CDs, cassettes, books and instruments. They have guitars, drum sets, recorders, xylophones and more. Just a few of the videos they offer are The Wind In The Willows, Tom Sawyer, Wildlife Symphony and Beatrix Potter's

The Tailor of Gloucester. Their cassettes and CDs are for **all ages**.

Spizzirri Publishing, Inc.

Post Office Box 9397
Rapid City, South Dakota 57709
800-322-9819

Call for a catalog of beautifully drawn coloring books filled with depictions of planets, transportation, birds, fish, dinosaurs, dolls and more. They offer Maze books, Dot-to-Dot and award winning color book and cassette kits on Planets, Dinosaurs, Cats of the Wild, Southeast Indians and Whales for **ages 2 to 10**.

The Timestables of History

Simon & Schuster/Touchstone
Rockefeller Center
1230 Avenue of the Americas
New York, New York 10020

The Timestables of History is a reference to world culture and history from 4500 B.C. to the present day. It covers the history of politics, literature, theatre, religion, philosophy, learning, visual arts, music, science, technology and daily life. The unique layout of the book juxtaposes the various subjects on a timeline which gives the reader an understanding of the events that occured each year around the world. Search the internet bookstore, Amazon.com at http://www.Amazon.com.

Nature Materials

American Forests

8555 Plummer Road
Jacksonville, Florida 32219
800-320-8733
904-765-0727

American Forests has a catalog of trees with a history. Did you know the Navajo-Apache people planted over 12,000 cottonwood trees as a future timber source or that the thousands of cherry trees that surround the Tidal Basin in Washington, D.C. were a gift from Japanese Emperor Mutsushito? This catalog of Famous and Historic Trees also has Famous and Historic Seeds. The classroom seed kit includes seeds, growing pots, instructions and a Living Classrooms Teacher's Guide with 45 pages of lessons and activities for children **ages 5 and up**.

Ampersand Press

750 Lake Street
Port Townsend, Washington 98368
800-624-4263
Fax 360-379-0324

Ampersand Press has a delightful selection of science and nature games and wildlife stamps for **ages 8 and up**. The beautifully illustrated Garden Game teaches players about gardening for food and the nature of soil, seeds and plants. A few card games they offer are The Bug Game, Onto The Desert, Predator, Oh Wilderness and Krill. The AC/DC card game teaches children **ages 8 and up** about electrical circuitry through simple illustrations.

Gardens For Growing People

Post Office Box 630
Point Reyes, California 94956-0630
415-663-9433

Gardens For Growing People is a fantastic catalog of ideas and products for children **ages 3 and up** to enjoy gardening. The catalog offers garden based curriculum, gardening books and videos, science and ecology, art and music, games, composting and even history. How can gardens involve a lesson in history? You can make living history by growing the same vegetables the Native Americans grew like Seneca Red Stalk Corn or Black Turtle Bush Bean. They also have seeds that will grow into flowers known to attract butterflies or birds.

GEMS

Lawrence Hall of Science
University of California
Berkeley, California 94720
510-642-7771
Fax 510-643-0309

Mapping Animal Movements and *Mapping Fish Habitats* are just two of the numerous publications offered by the Lawrence Hall of Science for **grades 6 and up**. The materials include lesson plans, activities, instructions on how to prepare and conduct the lessons, a list of materials and background information.

National Gardening Association

180 Flynn Avenue
Burlington, Vermont 05401
800-538-7476 (LETSGRO)
Fax 800-863-5962

> *GrowLab: A Complete Guide to Gardening in the Classroom* and *GrowLab: Activities for Growing Minds* are gardening resource and activity books for **grades K through 6**. Call for more information on the publications by The National Gardening Association including *Growing Ideas*, a journal of garden-based learning.

National Geographic Society

1145 17th Street N.W.
Washington, D.C. 20036-4688
800-368-2728
800-447-0647 Customer Service

> The National Geographic Society has catalogs of products for **ages 2 and up**. Call and ask for a member catalog of books, videos and craft kits or a catalog of maps, globes and atlases. The catalog features mural maps that are 110" x 76". The National Geographic Society also features the National Geographic Kids Network, a computer-based science curriculum that focuses on acid rain, nutrition, solar energy, trash, water quality and weather. Students in

grades 4 through 6 explore real-world scientific issues and exchange information with students around the world.

The Nature Company

750 Hearst Avenue.
Berkeley, California 94710
800-227-1114

> The Nature Company is a retail store for children of **all ages** and adults. It offers a variety of books and projects including nature videos from the Discovery Channel and The Raise and Release Butterfly Kit. The Nature Company also offers information on nature adventure trips. Call to receive a catalog or to find the nearest store.

NatureScope

National Wildlife Federation
8925 Leesburg Pike
Vienna, Virginia 22184
800-432-6564

> The National Wildlife Federation offers curricula and materials for **grades K through 6**. Students learn about habitat destruction and conservation and the process of extinction through activities that integrate science with social studies, mathematics, drama, art and music.

Santa Barbara Botanic Garden

1212 Mission Canyon Road
Santa Barbara, California 93105-2199
805-682-4726

> The Botanic garden features curricula for elementary school students. A few of the activity based resource guides are *Happenin' Habitats* for **grades 3 through 8** and the *Nature Kit: From Seeds to Sprouts* for **grades K through 6**. Activity pages are offered in English and Spanish. Call for a flier listing the publications offered.

Wildlife Education

9820 Willow Creek Road Suite 300
San Diego, California 92131-1112
800-477-5034
Fax 619-578-9658

> Wildlife Education offers the *Zoobooks* series of soft cover books featuring over fifty animals and a CD-ROM. Each book includes facts and photos on a different animal such as a koala or a zebra.

Wild Planet Toy Company

Post Office Box 194077
San Francisco, California 94119-4087
800-247-6570

> Wild Planet produces nature discovery toys for children including the MegaScope for **ages 5 to 10**. Call for a catalog or ask where you can find their products.

LANGUAGE ARTS MATERIALS

Academic Therapy Publications

High Noon Books - Ann Arbor Division
20 Commercial Boulevard
Novato, California 94949-6191
800-442-7249
415-883-3314
http://www.atpub.com

> Academic Therapy Publications offers supplementary curriculum materials focusing on spelling, cursive writing, perceptual activities, comprehension, thought and word tracking, self-esteem, math and more for **1st grade reading level and up**. High Noon Books, a division of Academic Publications, has a great catalog of books on exciting subjects such as great medical milestones, biographies of sports and entertainment stars, geography, roleplaying and math. Academic Therapy Publications also offers materials for special education classrooms, ESL and adult literacy programs.

Audio Forum

96 Broad Street
Guilford, Connecticut 06437
800-243-1234
203-453-9794
Fax 203-453-9774

> Audio Forum's Tapes for Business catalog includes a

selection of programs to build vocabulary, grammar, spelling and speech skills.

Chinaberry

2780 Via Orange Way Suite B

Spring Valley, California 91978

800-776-2242

Fax 619-670-5203

Foreign orders & non-customer service 619-670-5200

The Chinaberry has a wonderful selection of books for children of **all ages** including adults. Just a few examples of the selection are The Market Guide for Young Writers, Babe The Gallant Pig, and What Is God? Chinaberry also hosts fund-raiser book fairs for their customers. Call or write to receive a book fair packet.

Leap Frog

2608 9th Street

Berkeley, California 94710

800-701-5327

Leap Frog produces a Phonics Learning System designed with the assistance of Dr. Robert Calfee and Kristy Dunlap of the Stanford University Graduate School of Education. Children place a magnetic letter in the correct space on the word card and the game reads the word aloud. If they press the letter, "D" on the word card children will hear the correct phonetic sound, "Da". **Ages 3 and up.** They also offer lessons for the desk and for traveling. Call for a catalog.

The Learning Crew

571 W. 9320 S.

Sandy, Utah 84070

800-386-8673

http://www.lgcy.com/tlc

The Learning Crew produces a reading program called Challenger Phonics Fun. This program includes videos and reading kits designed to encourage beginning readers and is recommended for **ages 2 to adult**. Call for a brochure.

Orchard Hill Productions

2397 N.W. Kings Boulevard #308

Coryallis, Oregon 97330

800-811-5372

http://www.ohp.com

Orchard Hill Productions produces Word Clue Adventure for **ages 4 to 8**. This 30 minute live action video tape comes complete with its own companion activity book. Aside from winning several honors, Word Clue Adventure also has its own web site where eager participants can hear sound clips and learn more about this product.

Of all those arts in which the wise excel,
Nature's chief masterpiece is writing well.
–John Sheffield, Essay on Poetry

SCIENCE AND MATH MATERIALS

The Backyard Scientist

Post Office Box 16966

Irvine, California 92713-6966

714-551-2392

Fax 714-552-5351

> The Backyard Scientist publishes the Backyard Scientist science activity books by Jane Hoffman. The series of books focuses on chemistry, physics, geology and earth science activities for children **ages 4 to 12**. The award winning books are educational and easy to read with fun illustrations.

Creative Publications

5623 W. 115th St.

Worth, Illinois 60482

800-642-0822

Fax 800-624-0821

> Creative Publications has a catalog of science and nature activities for children and teens in **pre-K through grade 12**. For example, *Seeds and Weeds* features 28 activities as well as listing a learning objective, process skills, questions for discussion and directions for the exploration.

Edmund Scientific Co.

101 E. Gloucester Pike

Barrington, New Jersey 08007-1380

609-547-8880

Fax 609-573-6295

Scientifics is a catalog of science products and kits designed for students and educators alike. **For ages 6 to adult**, their products include electronic robot kits, telescopes and a variety of science discovery toys. This company also offers a catalog for industrial optics which carries hand prepared microscope slides, garden soil test kits, acid rain test kits, an assortment of motors and much more. You might also want to take advantage of "SM14 The General Pattern of the Scientific Method" written by the founder of Edmund Scientific Co., Norman W. Edmund. This booklet illustrates a step by step process to problem solving and promotes the exploration of knowledge, goal planning and choosing a career.

Educational Design, Inc.

345 Hudson Street

New York, New York 10014

800-221-9372

Call for a catalog or to ask where their products are sold in your area. Educational design offers an intriguing variety of educational discovery kits and mini labs. **For ages 8 and older**, the kits include planetary science, home planetariums, aerodynamic experiments, electric motors, radios, chemistry, physics, a pocket science lab and a finger print kit. For children **ages 4 and older**, they have a specialized line called Playground Science.

Eureka

Lawrence Hall of Science, University of California, Berkeley, California 94720-5200

510-642-1016

The Lawrence Hall of Science has been developing teaching materials for over 25 years. Eureka is a catalog of activities and teaching materials focusing on topics such as astronomy, math, science and biology. It is an endless list of activities for students in **grades k through 12** to experience hands-on learning.

The Exploratorium

3601 Lyon Street

San Francisco, California 94123

415-561-0393

http://www.exploratorium.edu/

The Exploratorium is a science and discovery museum designed to delight both children and adults. Call to receive their catalog which includes childrens science and discovery tools and several books which offer fantastic science projects for **ages 8 to adult**.

What is now proved was once only imagined.
—William Blake, The Marriage of Heaven and Hell

Hands-On Equations

Borenson and Associates

Post Office Box 3328

Allentown, Pennsylvania 18106

800-993-6284

610-398-6908

> Hands-On Equations is an approach that uses game pieces to physically present an algebraic equation to students in **grades 3 to adult**. Players can use moves to physically solve the equation.

National Sciences Resource Center

Arts and Industries Building, Room 1201

Smithsonian Institution

Washington, D.C. 20560

> The NSRC is a joint operation by the National Academy of Sciences and the Smithsonian Institution to help school districts develop and sustain hands-on science programs. *Resources for Teaching Elementary School Science* is a reference book by the NRSC which references curriculum materials, professional associations, science activity books, supplementary materials, U.S. government organizations, museums and other places to visit that focus on earth, life, physical and applied science.
>
> Search the online bookstore, Amazon.com, at http://www.Amazon.com.

OWI Incorporated

1160 Mahalo Place
Compton, California 90220-5443
800-638-4732
310-638-7970
http://www.owirobot.com/

>Call to receive their catalog of robot kits including characters like the award winning Hyper Peppy for children **ages 10 to 12**. They also offer Robotics and Electricity Technology Curriculum as well as 99 Electronics Experiments kit in English and Spanish.

Scientific American

415 Madison Avenue
New York, New York 10017
800-333-1199
515-247-7631

>Scientific American is a great magazine that reports on the latest scientific discoveries and inventions. Scientific American, Inc. also has a catalog of products including books and CD-ROMs.

The Scientific Revolution

#6 Stanford Shopping Center
Palo Alto, California 94304
415-322-1876

>The Scientific Revolution is a retail store and a division of the Nature Company that offers science related products for **all ages**. Currently, they have stores located in Los Angeles, CA; Palo Alto, CA; Berkeley,

CA; Boston, MA; Bloomington, MN and Baltimore, MD. Store locations may change so call to find the one nearest you.

S & J Products International, Inc.

Lyndale Books, Inc.
Post Office Box 1203
Palatine, Illinois 60078
708-358-8870
Fax 708-358-9910

> S & J Products International, Inc. has a series of materials used to teach mathematical and science concepts as well as stimulate imagination for levels **preK through grade 12**. Their titles include *Basic Math Concepts* and the *Mother Goose And Then Some* series using Mother Goose Rhymes to spark creativity and expressive skills. These titles are distributed by Lyndale Books, Incorporated.

Tobin's Lab

Post Office Box 6503
Glendale, Arizona 85312-6503
800-522-4776
602-843-4265
http://www.tobinlab.com/

> Tobin's Lab is a catalog of hands-on science materials for families. They have products that introduce children and teens **ages 4 to 16** to electricity, microbiology, dissection, magnets, specimens, plants and seeds, space, water, physics, color, solar power, astronomy and so much more.

TransTech

Creative Learning Systems, Inc.
16510 Via Esprillo
San Diego, California 92127-1708
800-458-2880
Fax 619-675-7707

The Trans Tech catalog is filled with technological products that reflect our fast paced world of science and electronics. A few of the subjects represented for **ages 6 to adult** are edutainment, entrepreneurship, robotics, flight and creativity. Science kits and books aren't the only products you'll discover. They also have such advanced systems as a Jet Stream 500 Wind Tunnel.

Twin Sisters Productions

1340 Home Avenue Suite D
Akron, Ohio 44310-2570
800-248-8946

Twin Sisters Productions offers a wide variety of affordably priced educational books and cassettes on astronomy, chemistry, paleontology, entomology, marine biology, meteorology, physics, zoology, phonics, math, foreign languages, safety, social studies, letters and numbers, colors and shapes and more. A few examples of their titles are Division-Rap With The Facts, I'd like to be an Astronaut and States & Capitals. Their products are appropriate for **ages 2 to 10**.

SAFETY MATERIALS

Child Lures, Ltd.
2119 Shelburne Road
Shelburne, Vermont 05482
802-985-8458
http://www.childlures.com/
> Child Lures Prevention Program is a five part program that comprehensively addresses child sexual abuse and includes a family guide, TV news series, seminars and a program for schools.

Davis Productions
141 New Road
Parsippany, New Jersey 07054
201-808-1144
> Baby Proof Home is a 40 minute video on a room by room tour to help locate potential hazards so that you can better protect your baby at home.

Insurance Institute For Highway Safety
1005 North Giebe Road
Arlington, Virginia 22201
703-247-1500
http://www.hwysafety.org/
> Learn how to protect children in vehicles equipped with airbags. The video titled Kids And Airbags demonstrates correct infant and child restraint use to ensure optimum protection.

LifeSmart

800-471-5760

StrangerSmart is an award winning, informative and straightforward video that teaches children and adults how to avoid becoming a victim of kidnapping and other crimes.

One Step Ahead

Post Office Box 517
Lake Bluff, Illinois 60044
800-274-8440

One Step Ahead is a catalog of products ranging from toys to strollers for infants and toddlers . They have a selection of outdoor and swimming safety products such as helmets and protection against swimmer's ear.

Perfectly Safe

7835 Freedom Avenue NW
North Canton, Ohio 44720-6907
800-837-KIDS
Fax 330-492-8290

Perfectly Safe is a catalog of hundreds of safety products for prenatal through preschool years. Outlets with built in child barriers, corner and edge cushions, stove guards and child size toilet seats are just a few of the products Perfectly Safe has to offer.

Raya Systems

2570 West El Camino Real Suite 520

Mountain View, California 94040

800-276-4376

> Bronkie the Bronchiasaurus is a video game for children and adolescents featuring "Bronkie" who battles asthma triggers, takes daily medication, uses an inhaler and monitors his peak flow. The game features 24 levels, a two player option and can be played in English and Spanish.
>
> Packy and Marlon is a video game for children ages 8 to 15 on how to manage diabetes. The game entails monitoring their blood glucose levels, choosing an insulin plan, and planning a healthy and balanced diet. The game also touches on the basics of diabetes self care and how to handle typical social situations. The game features a two player option and can be played in English and Spanish.

Safe-T-Child, Inc.

401 Friday Mountain Road

Austin, Texas 78737

512-288-2882

http://www.yellodyno.com/

> This program offers personal safety educational products and recovery skills. They feature a do-it-yourself child I.D. kit, cassettes with educational safety songs and educational books on how to keep your child safe.

Safety Belt Safe U.S.A.

Post Office Box 553

Altadena, California 91003

800-745-SAFE

> This is a non-profit organization that offers a bimonthly Safety Belt Safe News, a quarterly Safe Ride Newsletter and a membership program. They also feature a list of resources and tips for parents and educators on how to keep you and your children safe plus positive ways to teach passenger safety to young children.

SBS Prevention Plus

649 Main Street, Suite B

Groveport, Ohio 43125

800-858-5222

Fax 614-836-8359

> Don't Shake The Baby is a program that introduces the dangers of shaking babies to decrease the resulting incidence of blindness, disability and death. It was produced by the Ohio Research Institute of Child Abuse Prevention and includes a video, posters, public service announcements and other print materials. The SBS has also developed Child Behavior Management Cards which are 5"x 8" cards used to improve knowledge about behavioral and developmental expectations of children and nonviolent approaches to child behavior management.

Substance Abuse Education, Inc.

670 S. 4th Street

Edwardsville, Kansas 66113

800-530-5607

913-441-1868

Fax 913-441-2119

Safety First: A Guide to Safe Child Care is a computer software program for adolescents and young adults who baby-sit. It provides information on how to deal with medical emergencies such as minor burns, poisoning, choking, nosebleeds, cuts and bruises. SAE has a software series on drug abuse prevention, health and guidance. Call for more information.

AWARENESS MATERIALS

The Advocates for Youth

Suite200
1025 Vermont Avenue., N.W.
Washington, D.C. 20005
202-347-5700
Fax 202-347-2263

Talking with TV is a booklet designed to teach parents and other adults how to use TV to spark discussions with children and teens about values, relationships, sexuality and other issues portrayed on TV. The booklet is updated annually to focus on current TV shows. The price is $4.00.

Balducci Productions

23-00 Route 208 South
Fair Lawn, New Jersey 07410
800-881-5235
201-703-1750

The Hospital Adventures of Jimmy, Judy & AC is a video about a young boy and his animated friend. They follow a little girl through her stay at the hospital. This video for ages 4 to 9 is cleverly designed to put a patient's anxiety to rest. Balducci also produces Hector, Maria and AC Meet the Germs. This video teaches children about bacteria and the virus and what kids can do to stay healthy. Kids learn how germs can get into a person's body and how to stay healthy by getting a lot of sleep, exercising, eating right and staying clean.

Center for Media Education

202-628-2620

It's the Law is a video that explores the influences of television on children of all ages and explains how the Children's Television Act of 1990 can help improve the quality of children's programming.

The Center for Media Literacy

4727 Wilshire Boulevard
Los Angeles, California 90010
800-226-9494

Parenting in a TV Age is a curriculum kit designed to educate parents about the issues television brings into the lives of children of all ages. The program teaches how to set limits on TV, cope with commercials, set standards for violent content and more. Call to order a brochure or to receive more information on media literacy in general.

Children's Action Network

10951 W. Pico Boulevard
Los Angeles, California 90064
310-470-9599
Fax 310-474-9665

Through Our Eyes is a film portraying the children's perspective on problems such as violence, drugs, homelessness and pollution as they are seen and experienced by today's youth.

Jason & Nordic Publishers

424 Montgomery Street, Post Office Box 441
Hollidaysburg, Pennsylvania 16648-1432
814-696-2920

> Turtle Books are a series of 11 books, each on a different disability, that support an understanding of children with disabilities. The books, designed for elementary and grade school children, promote self-acceptance and overcoming obstacles.

Necessary Pictures Film & Media

Post Office Box 107, Old Chelsea Station
New York, New York 10011-0107
800-221-3170

> My Hair's Falling Out... Am I Still Pretty? A Childhood Cancer Education Video is a 22 minute story about two children with cancer who are hospital roommates. The video explains hospital procedures, tests and the effects of chemotherapy. The feeling of the video is friendly and informative and is appropriate for use in 4th through 12th grade classrooms.

SPECIAL NEEDS MATERIALS

Academic Therapy Publications
High Noon Books - Ann Arbor Division
20 Commercial Boulevard
Novato, California 94949-6191
800-442-7249
415-883-3314
http://www.atpub.com

> Academic Therapy Publications offers a catalog of materials for special education preK through adult classrooms. The catalog resources include basic skills tests, supplementary curriculum, parent/teacher techniques and visual remediation materials.

Alexander Graham Bell Association for the Deaf Inc.
3417 Volta Place NW
Washington D.C. 20007-2778
202-337-5220

> They offer services and support for the deaf including training, conferences, scholarships, awards and a catalog of books, software and reference materials.

American Foundation for the Blind
11 Penn Plaza Suite 300
New York, New York 10001-2018
212-620-2000

> They offer assistance and referral services for the visually impaired. They have one of the most exten-

sive libraries on blindness in the world.

American Speech-Language Hearing Association
10801 Rockville Pike
Rockville, Maryland 20852
800-638-8255
Helpline 800-638-8255
> Call the helpline for information on speech and hearing disorders and referrals for speech-language pathologists and audiologists.

The Council for Exceptional Children
1920 Association Drive, Dept. K7022
Reston, Virginia 20191-1589
800-232-7323
703-264-9446
Fax 703-264-1637
http://www.cec.sped.org/home.htm
> The Council for Exceptional Children catalog features professional products and training for students with special needs and teachers in special education classrooms. They have conventions, workshops, training guides and periodicals such as Exceptional Child Resources, Exceptional Children, Behavioral Disorders and Career Development for Exceptional Individuals.

Learning disAbilities Resources

Post Office Box 716

Bryn Mawr, Pennsylvania 19010

800-869-8336

610-525-8336

Fax 610-525-8337

> This catalog of resources for the learning disabled includes a language development series, spelling workbooks, study aids, teaching aids, motivational items and videos for parents and teachers. They also offer a newsletter and a list of workshops.

March of Dimes

Birth Defects Foundation, National Headquarters

1275 Mamaroneck Avenue

White Plains, New York 10605

914-428-7100

800-367-6630

> The March of Dimes works to improve the health of babies by preventing birth defects. They have a Catalog of Public Health Education Materials which cover topics such as prenatal care, environmental hazards, genetics and teen pregnancy.

Muscular Dystrophy Association

114 Old Country Road Suite 116

Mineola, New york 11501

718-793-1100

> They support research for treatments for muscular dystrophy and related neuromuscular disorders. They also offer assistance in finding orthopedic

appliances, daily living aids, flu shots, career counseling and educational and recreational activities.

National Organization for Rare Disorders, Inc.

Post Office Box 8923
New Fairfield, Connecticut 06812-8923
800-999-6673
203-746-6518
Fax 203-746-6481

This federation of voluntary health organizations is
dedicated to helping people with rare "orphan" dis-
eases. NORD provides information on over 5,000
rare disorders and referrals to additional sources of
assistance and ongoing support.

Rifton

Post Office Box 901, Route 213
Rifton, New York 12471-0901
800-777-4244
Fax 800-336-5948
International Access Fax 914-658-8065

Rifton develops therapeutic equipment for handi-
capped children and adults. A few of their products
are dynamic standers, tricycles, gait trainers, lift walk-
ers, advancement chairs, supine boards, toddler
chairs and easels.

SCHOOL CATALOGS

The majority of the companies and organizations in this section specialize in supplying schools and home schoolers with materials for the classroom although many of these companies are happy to make sales to individuals as well.

American Home-School Publishing

5310 Affinity Ct.
Centreville, Virginia 22020
703-266-0348
http://www.ahsp.com/

This online catalog offers discount prices on products from over 40 publishers. The topics range from architecture, art, bible stories and games, biography, curriculum guides, english language arts, literature, ethics, virtue, morality, fitness, health, educational games, reference, geography, history, mathematics, music, science, engineering, U.S. government and foreign languages; french, german, russian, and spanish. You can order a printed catalog by calling or visiting their web site or you can take advantage of their online catalog which includes age recommendations and thumbnail pictures of the products you desire.

Association for Supervision and Curriculum Development

1250 N. Pitt Street

Alexandria, Virginia 22314-1453

800-933-2723

703-549-9110

Fax 703-299-8631

http://www.ascd.org/

> The ASCD is an organization of educators that offers a membership and products. The membership includes a newsletter, *Education Update* and a supplement. The supplement, *Curriculum Update*, reports trends, research, exemplary programs and resources available in individual subjects. ASCD's products include books focusing on positive classroom environments, helping urban schools, grant proposals and more. They also have a line of Professional Inquiry Kits for school improvement teams and study groups. The kits provide new ideas in curriculum, instruction and assessment.

The Big Deal Book

Marketing Projects, Inc.

3800 N. Wilke Rd. Ste. 300

Arlington Hts., Illinois 60004

800-650-0034

847-670-0034

Fax 847-670-0042

> The Big Deal Book is a must have book of discounts, coupons and free materials for K through 8 educators. It contains discounts on resource books, class-

room decor, magazines, software, seminars, association memberships plus they offer The Big Deal Book of Technology for K through 12 educators.

Biotech Publishing

Post Office Box 1032
Angleton, Texas 77516-1032
713-369-2044

> Biotech Publishing offers science books on plant biotechnologies, unique experiments with seeds, making hands-on science easy, science fairs and how to write a science research paper.

Cannon Sports

Post Office Box 11179
Burbank, California 91510-1179
800-223-0064
818-771-5201
Fax 800-223-0064

> Footballs, basketballs, volleyballs, waterpolo balls, archery accessories, badminton rackets, baseball plates, exercise and weightlifting equipment, gymnastic folding mats, hockey kits, lacrosse supplies, athletic apparel and stadium equipment are just a fraction of what the Cannon Sports catalog has to offer. They provide equipment for nearly every sport offered in schools. They sell to companies, institutions and individuals.

Center for Applied Research in Education

110 Brookhill Drive

West Nyack, New York 10995

The Center for Applied Research in Education produces several innovative books such as Brain Games and Ready-To-Use Social Skills Lessons & Activities. The Ready-To-Use Social Skills Lessons & Activities book has two levels, grades 4 through 6 and 7 through 12. Both editions involve decision making, problem-solving, developing self-control, understanding rules, resisting group pressure, setting career goals and much more. Brain Games is a resource of over 170 entertaining activities designed to develop critical and creative thinking for students in grades 6 through 12. Activities involve language arts, math, science, social studies, careers, values and the media.

Childcraft Education Corp.

Post Office Box 3239

Lancaster, Pennsylvania 17604

800-631-5652

Fax 888-532-4453

http://www.childcrafteducation.com/

Childcraft manufactures a variety of classroom furniture and shelving units. They also carry wood blocks, giant soft blocks, washable paints, books, musical instruments, globes, gardening kits, resources for teachers who educate young children and much more.

Chime Time

One Sportime Way
Atlanta, Georgia 30340
800-477-5075
770-449-5700
Fax 800-845-1535

> Chime Time is a catalog of movement products for preschool and elementary students. Their products include balance builders, trampolines, jump ropes, adjustable hurdles, foam shapes and mats, building blocks, rhythm band sets, activity and dance videos, furniture, outdoor play sets and much more.

Community Playthings

Post Office Box 500
Norfolk, Connecticut 06058-0500
800-777-4244
Fax 800-336-5948

> Community Playthings offers a wide range of maple furniture and play sets such as kitchens and construction sites for ages 2 to 8. Their giant hollow blocks measuring 5 1/2" x 11" x 22" exercise the mind and body.

100% Educational Videos

Post Office Box 775
Orangevale, California 95662
800-483-3383
Fax 916-987-7936

> Peer pressure, eating disorders, puberty, self-esteem and psychoactive drugs are just a few of the topics

discussed in the health videos from 100% Educational Videos. They are intended for students in grades 5 and up.

Environments, Inc.

Post Office Box 1348, Beaufort Industrial Park
Beaufort, South Carolina 29901-1348
800-EI-CHILD
803-846-8155
Fax 800-EI-FAX-US

> Environments is a great catalog of educational products focusing on fine motor skills, language arts, mathematics, science and creative expression. It carries furniture, giant soft blocks and balls and an incredible selection of books including the classics at great prices. Environments, Inc. supplies to individuals and institutions.

Films For The Humanities and Sciences

Post Office Box 2053
Princeton, New Jersey 08543-2053
800-257-5126
609-275-1400
Fax 609-275-3767

> Films For The Humanities and Sciences has a catalog of health videos and videodiscs for educators, teens and adults. Just a few of the subjects represented are AIDS, allergies and asthma, attention deficit disorder, autism, child development, first-aid, health care professions, medical care and trends, mental health, speech and surgical procedures. They also offer a

rental program.

Free Loan Program

Gospel Films, Inc.
Post Office Box 455
Muskegon, Michigan 49443-0455
Fax 616-777-7598
http://www.freemedia.org

> This leading non-profit producer and distributor of free films for use in junior and senior high schools offers videos that focus on topics such as coaching, decision making, peer pressure, self-esteem, racial differences, intimacy, depression, religious faith and substance abuse.

Greenhaven Press, Inc.

Post Office Box 289009
San Diego, California 92198-9009
800-231-5163
Fax 619-485-9549

> Greenhaven Press publishes a Literary Companion series of books on American and world authors for young adults. Each book focuses on a particular author and includes a chronology of the author's life, an in-depth biography, summaries on the author's themes and insights provided for each essay and essay introductions which provide a guide for comprehending the main ideas. Greenhaven Press also publishes *Opposing Viewpoints* series for grades 4 through 12 which present controversial topics with pros and cons to promote discussion on the issue.

Greenhaven sells to schools, institutions and individuals.

Guidance Associates

Post Office Box 1000
Mount Kisco, New York 10549-0010
800-431-1242
Fax 914-666-5319

Guidance Associates have a video catalog of programs that focus on numerous topics some of which are American and world history, art, computer literacy, careers and job skills, government, journalism, literature, math, mythology, nutrition, peer pressure, science, substance abuse and suicide prevention.

The Health Connection

55 West Oak Ridge Drive
Hagerstown, Maryland
800-548-8700
Fax 301-790-9733
http://www.healthconnection.org/healthconnection/index.html

The Health Connection is a non-profit organization dedicated to producing and distributing educational tools to help children and teens. Their catalog features high quality curricula, counseling and support group materials that focus on topics such as drug awareness, nutrition, tobacco, grief, violence prevention, conflict resolution and AIDS. They have counseling tools for all ages from preK through grade 12. The Health Connection also offers strategies and techniques for educators and parents.

Health Edco

Post Office Box 21207
Waco, Texas 76702-1207
800-299-3366 Extension 295
Fax 888-977-7653

> Health Edco is a catalog of wellness tools such as videos, displays, curricula and programs that focus on lifestyle health education, nutrition, men's health, women's health, sexuality and drug and smoking prevention. They also have a large selection of anatomy models.

Human Kinetics

Post Office Box 5076
Champaign, Illinois 61825-5076
800-747-4457
Canada 800-465-7301
Calls outside U.S. and Canada 217-351-5076
http://www.humankinetics.com/

> Human Kinetics Catalogs feature informational products for physical activity-based professions. There are four different catalogs, each with its own group of products. The Human Kinetics Academic & Professional Resources catalog covers all fields of study in the sport and exercise sciences. It also covers professions such as cardiopulmonary rehabilitation, dance and sport management. The Human Kinetics Sports & Coaching catalog has information on coaching education, sports administration, multi-

sport training and specific sports. The Human Kinetics Fitness & Health catalog would be of interest to fitness professionals, fitness enthusiasts, and health promotion professionals. The Human Kinetics Physical Education, Recreation & Dance catalog features hands-on resources for preK through 12 educators and recreation and dance professionals.

Jordan's Knowledge Nook

2400 Judson Road
Longview, Texas 75605
800-562-5490
903-753-8741
Fax 903-757-6980

Jordan's Knowledge Nook has an extensive catalog of board games, books, activity books, maps, crafts, decorations and kits covering arts and crafts, geography, language arts, math, motivational, music, reading and science for grades preK to grade 8. They also have a selection of furniture and accessories.

Landmark Media Inc.

3450 Slade Run Drive
Falls Church, Virginia 22042
800-342-4336
703-241-2030
Fax 703-536-9540
From Canada 800-541-7713

This catalog of educational videos is filled with journeys into Thailand, Japan, the Himalayas and other exciting travels. The videos designed for classroom use and covers such subjects as the Bible, business, disabilities, drug abuse, economics, elementary math, algebra, calculus, geometry, trigonometry, probability and statistics, famous authors, geography, health, history, multicultures, reading, safaris and space. The average cost per video is $195.00 and rental videos are available at $65 per title. The catalog has a large selection of videos that challenge ages five to adult.

Math Teachers Press, Inc.

5100 Gamble Drive, Suite 398
Minneapolis, Minnesota 55416
800-852-2435
612-545-6535
Fax 612-545-6326

Math Teachers Press is a catalog of hands-on math activity books and programs using manipulatives such as miniature cubes, teddy bears, dinosaurs and scales to convey abstract math concepts to children in pre-kindergarten through high school. They sell to individuals and schools.

National Association for the Education of Young Children

1509 16th Street, N.W.
Washington, DC 20036-1426
800-424-2460
202-232-8777
Fax 202-328-1846
http://www.naeyc.org/naeyc

Call for an Early Childhood Resources Catalog. This catalog has products that cover a host of subjects such as health, nutrition, safety, science and technology, the arts, working with parents, social, moral and emotional development and more. They carry books, videos, brochures and kits.

National Sciences Resource Center

Arts and Industries Building, Room 1201
Smithsonian Institution
Washington, D.C. 20560

The NSRC is a joint operation by the National Academy of Sciences and the Smithsonian Institution to help school districts develop and sustain hands-on science programs. *Resources for Teaching Elementary School Science* is a reference book by the NRSC which references curriculum materials, professional associations, science activity books, supplementary materials, U.S. government organizations, museums and other places to visit that focus on earth, life, physical and applied science.

Search the internet bookstore, Amazon.com at http://www.Amazon.com.

Odyssey of the Mind School Program

Post Office Box 547

Glassboro, New Jersey 08028-0547

609-881-1603

Fax 609-881-3596

> The Odyssey of the Mind, Inc. is a non-profit corporation dedicated to developing creative problem-solving skills in students from kindergarten through college. Elementary schools, colleges, community group, home schools, military and individuals may become a member of the OM association. Members receive creative problem-solving activities, curriculum, the OM newsletter, a handbook and the option of entering team competition. Members come from around the world, including North America, Australia, China, Europe, Japan and South America.

Scholastic Inc.

2931 E. McCarty St.

Jefferson City, Missouri 65101

800-631-1586

http://www.scholastic.com

http://www.scholastic.ca   Sholastic Canada

> Call for a catalog of skills books, magazines, videos and professional materials for educators and home schoolers teaching grades 1 through 12. Scholastic's materials cover math, reading, art, culture, foreign languages and much more. Educators and home schoolers will find such books as Phonics For Learning Language, You and Your Body (teaches health habits), Be a Scientist, Real Life Employment,

Real Life Communication At Work and more. They also have book clubs for levels preschool through 9th grade. Visit their web site to find K through 8 core and supplemental programs and literacy activities for students.

School Specialty

609 Silver Street
Post Office Box 3004
Agawam, Massachusetts 01001-8004
800-628-8608
413-786-9800
Fax 413-789-4277 Or 800-272-0101
http://www.schoolspecialty.com

School Specialty has a general catalog and an arts and crafts catalog. The general catalog covers classroom supplies, reading, science, math, writing, history, geography, multicultural studies, physical education, coordination skills, art, crafts and even furniture. The Arts and Crafts catalog offers museum and great masters videos, brushes for oil, acrylics and ceramics, paints, airbrush supplies, furniture, paper, ceramic glazes, potter's wheels, kilns, beads, hand tools and more.

Silver Burdett Ginn

4350 Equity Drive, Post Office Box 2649
Columbus, Ohio 43216
800-848-9500

This is a catalog of products designed for educators and librarians. Individuals requesting teaching materials delivered to a home address need to supply a copy of a teaching certificate. Silver Burdett Ginn offers individual and classroom kit prices for books, videos, tapes and CDs in the areas of social studies, science, reading, language arts, music and mathematics for grades K through 8.

LANGUAGE TOOLS

These books can supplement any class or tutorial. Ask your local library if they can find a book in the language in which you are interested or search the internet bookstore, www.amazon.com.

The Cat in the Hat Beginner Book Dictionary in French

This book is published by Random House, Inc. The layout consists of words and short sentences in English with the translation in French. Each sentence has an accompanying illustration.

The Cat in the Hat Beginner Book Dictionary in Spanish

This book is published by Random House, Inc. The layout consists of words and short sentences in English with the translation in Spanish. Each sentence has a corresponding illustration.

Greek Heritage Dictionary

The Greek Heritage Dictionary c. 1989 Editions Renyl Inc. is a basic vocabulary book with an illustration, the word and then the Greek translation.

Green Eggs and Ham by Dr. Seuss

This book is available in English with the Chinese translation.

An Illustrated History of Korea Series

An Illustrated History of Korea book series by Samseong Publishing Co., Ltd. c. 1992 features photos and text describing Korea's history and is written in Korean for the secondary school level.

Let's Speak French! A First Book of Words

This is a vocabulary book with colorful illustrations, the word and the French translation. Published by The Penguin Group, New York, New York, 1993.

My First Spanish Word Book

http://www.dk.com

My First Spanish Word Book is a Dorling Kindersley Book. Featuring photographs with the English word and the Spanish translation.

Alcazar Music

Post Office Box 429, South Maine Street
Waterbury, Vermont 05676
800-541-9904
Fax 802-244-6128

Alcazar Music's master catalog has a series of French/English, German/English, Italian/English and Spanish/English lyric language books with cassettes. Also see page 28.

American Home-School Publishing

5310 Affinity Ct.

Centreville, Virginia 22020

703-266-0348

http://www.ahsp.com/

>This online catalog offers discount prices on products from over 40 publishers. The have foreign language programs in French, German, Russian and Spanish. You can order a printed catalog by calling or visiting their web site or you can take advantage of their online catalog which includes age recommendations and thumbnail pictures of the products you desire.

Audio Forum

96 Broad Street

Guilford, Connecticut 06437

800-243-1234

203-453-9794

Fax 203-453-9774

>Audio Forum's instructional language catalog includes programs in nearly 100 languages. A portion of the comprehensive list includes languages of Africa, Asia, Central Europe, Far East, India, Middle East, Native American, Eastern and Western Europe and classical languages. They have courses for **children and adults** and they also have the games Scrabble and Monopoly in French and Spanish.

Berlitz International

293 Wall St.

Princeton, New Jersey 08540

800-923-7548

http://www.berlitz.com

Berlitz International has a wide range of products to teach the language of your choice with a line especially designed for children called Berlitz Kids. *The Adventures With Nicholas* series includes an illustrated paperback book with a corresponding narrative audiocassette, a dictionary and songs that involve listening and speaking. The series is designed for **ages 4 to 7** and is printed in French, German, Italian or Spanish. Berlitz also carries language audiocassettes, guides and CD-ROMs available in many languages for **all ages** from students to business people.

Bueno

In One Ear

29481 Manzanita Drive

Campo, California 91906

Spanish is not the only language represented in this catalog. They also have products for **children and adults** that teach English, French, German, Italian, Japanese and Russian. The selection includes coloring books, cook books, activity books, videos, cassettes, software and children's book titles such as *Peter Rabbit* in French, Italian and Spanish.

Kimbo Educational

10 North Third Avenue
Post Office Box 477z
Long Branch, New Jersey 07740-0477
800-631-2187
Fax 908-870-3340
Outside the Continental U.S. 908-229-4949

Kimbo Educational is a catalog of educational musical products for **infants** and **children ages 3 to 15**. Musical lyrics are used to teach grammar, phonics, math, Spanish, French, German, Italian, Japanese, social skills and more. The majority of the CDs, cassettes and videos are accompanied by a guide. They also feature well priced nylon parachutes with handles and rhythmic parachute cassettes.

Language Connect

800-syrlang
http://www.syrlang.com

Language Connect has a series of CD-ROM software courses in a number of different languages. The All-in-One Language Fun course introduces children to five languages; Spanish, French, German, Japanese and English. Through games such as bingo, jigsaw puzzles, memory teasers and more, children learn 200 words and phrases in each language. They also have CD-ROMs for adults and a newsletter for language learners.

Language Publications Interactive

New York

800-882-6700

212-620-3193

Who Is Oscar Lake? is the title of a CD-ROM that frames you as a jewel thief in a live-action mystery. In order to leave the country and clear your name you must learn the language. It is available in English, French, German, Italian and Spanish. **Ages 8 and up**.

Penton Overseas, Inc.

2470 Impala Drive

Carlsbad, California 92008-7226

800-748-5804

619-431-0060

Fax 619-431-8110

Penton Overseas, Inc. produces language learning audio and video programs for **all ages**. Sound Beginnings, developed for a baby's first months, features nursery rhymes, words, phrases and traditional music in Spanish, French, German, Russian, Hebrew and Japanese. They also have a large selection of video and audio programs designed to teach children and adults colors, shapes, bilingual skills and conversation in English, French, German, Italian, Japanese and Spanish. Their language learning card games are also a fun way to improve your language skills.

Scholastic Inc.

2931 E. McCarty St.

Jefferson City, Missouri 65101

800-631-1586

> The magazine titles Scholastic offers in French, German and Spanish are Allons-Y!, Bonjour, Ça Va?, Chez Nous, ¿Qué Tal?, Ahora, El Sol, Das Rad, Schuss and Aktuell. The subscriptions are for classrooms and home schooling. For more information on Scholastic go to page 74.

Transparent Language

22 Proctor Hill Road

Post Office Box 575

Hollis, New Hampshire 03049-0575

800-752-1767

603-465-2230

Fax 603-465-2779

http://www.transparent.com

> The Transparent Language product series teaches a new language through famous literature, TV commercials and articles. The Language Now CD-ROM or diskette/audio cassette is available in English, French, German, Italian, Latin, Russian and Spanish for **ages 12 and up**.
>
> Word Ace is a CD-ROM dictionary containing more than 40,000 words and 500,000 verb conjugations. It is available in French, German, Italian, Latin, Russian, Spanish, European Portuguese, Brazilian Portuguese, Swedish, Dutch, Finnish, Danish and Norwegian.
>
> Transparent Language offers books on CD-ROM or

cassette in many languages and a Side Streets of the World series featuring a historical, architectural and cultural tour of a country. For more information, call or visit their web site.

Twin Sisters Productions
1340 Home Avenue Suite D
Akron, Ohio 44310-2570
800-248-8946

The "Listen and Learn a Language" series entertains children using cheerful melodies to incorporate learned words into a song. The 60 minute audiocassette and 24 page illustrated learning guide and lyric book teach over 100 words. Also available is a teacher reproducible book with crossword puzzles, art activities, bookmaking projects and coloring pages to make learning a new language fun. It is available in English, Spanish, French, German or Italian and priced under $10.00. Call for a catalog.

United Nations Children's Fund
Post Office Box 182233
Chattanooga, Tennessee 37422
800-553-1200
212-326-7000
Fax 212-888-7465

UNICEF publishes a perennial catalog of specialty products language building games such as Games Around the World which is published in English, French, Spanish and Portuguese and Lingo, a word game that teaches the names of food in eight languages. The United Nations Children Fund cooperates with governments in more than 140 countries to help provide clean water, health care, education and nutrition programs for children and mothers.

Usborne Books

http://www.usborne-books.com/
http://members.aol.com/debbymac/Usborne-USA/index.html

> Usborne has a series of books called The Usborne First Thousand Words available in English, French, German, Japanese and Spanish. They also have The First 100 Words sticker book available in Spanish, French or English. View their line of products at the web addresses above or search the Amazon.com online bookstore, at http://www.amazon.com.

English As A Second Language Home Page

http://www.lang.uiuc.edu/r-li5/esl/

> This web site offers resources such as online conversation books, audio programs, reading links, 11 rules of grammar, english punctuation, grammar and style notes, English language schools and more.

Human Languages Page

http://www.june29.com/HLP/

> A web site providing multilingual resources to learn, practice and study a particular language including spoken samples of a language.

MAGAZINES AND
NEWSPAPERS

The magazines are listed in order of the age of its intended audience, beginning with the youngest age group. Many publishers offer sample issues or information on where to find their magazine in your area. For special offers on magazines for individuals and classrooms, check The Big Deal Book for K through 8 educators. See page 63.

Babybug

The Cricket Magazine Group
Box 7434
Red Oak, Iowa 51591-2434
800-827-0227
http://www.musemag.com

> This magazine which features rhymes, stories and illustrations has rounded cardboard pages without staples making it a great choice for children **ages 6 months to 2 years**. It is published by Carus Publishing Company, The Cricket Magazine Group and a subscription includes 9 issues a year. See their web site for more information.

Ladybug

The Cricket Magazine Group
Box 7434
Red Oak, Iowa 51591-2434
800-827-0227
http://www.musemag.com

> Published by Carus Publishing Co., The Cricket Magazine Group, this magazine is filled with stories, poems, songs, games and activities designed for chil-

dren **ages 2 to 6**. A subscription includes 12 issues. See their web site for more information.

Sesame Street Magazine

Post Office Box 55518
Boulder, Colorado 80322-5518

This magazine offers a variety of educational games, stories and activities for children **ages 2 to 6**. It is published by the Children's Television Workshop. Schools and other institutions can order at bulk copy rates upon request.

Highlights for children

Highlights for children
Post Office Box 182051
Columbus, Ohio 43218-2051

For preschoolers: Preschoolers learn to think and analyze through matching games, puzzles and picture problems.

6 to 8-year-olds: Children learn to read through picture words and stories. There are puzzles, riddles and stories that stress values. It includes monthly "What's Wrong?" pictures which develop perception, attention span and vocabulary.

9 to 12-year-olds: Pre-teens can complete science projects and arts and crafts. Projects are designed so pre-teens can experiment safely on their own.

Your Big Backyard

National Wildlife Federation
Post Office Box 777
Mount Morris, Illinois 61054-0777
800-588-1650
http://www.nwf.org/nwf

> This magazine explores nature discovery and wildlife for preschoolers **ages 3 to 5**. It offers crafts, stories, facts, games and vivid photographs and is published monthly by the National Wildlife Federation.

Kid City

Post Office Box 53349
Boulder, Colorado 80322-1277

> *Kid City* is published by the Children's Television Workshop for children **ages 6 to 9**. It contains games and puzzles along with articles on current events, people and activities.

Kids Discover

Post Office Box 54205
Boulder, Colorado 80322-4205
212-242-5133

> This magazine uses beautiful photographs to visit exciting subjects and locations in each issue. The variety of previous topics including the Himalayas, Pyramids, the brain and earthquakes make this a wonderful choice for **ages 6 years and up**.

Ranger Rick

National Wildlife Federation

Post Office Box 777

Mount Morris, Illinois 61054-0777

800-588-1650

http://www.nwf.org/nwf

> This magazine explores nature discovery and wildlife for children **ages 6 to 12**. It offers crafts, stories, facts, photographs and games. It is published monthly by the National Wildlife Federation.

Spider, the magazine for children

Box 7435

Red Oak, Iowa 51591

800-827-0227

http://www.musemag.com

> This is a beautifully illustrated magazine featuring stories, poetry, articles and activities for boys and girls **ages 6 to 9**. Published by Carus Publishing Co., The Cricket Magazine Group. A one year subscription includes 12 issues. Go to the web site for more information.

Scienceland Inc.

501 Fifth Avenue., Ste. 2108

New York, New York 10017-6165

212-490-2180

> This is a beautifully illustrated magazine that features articles and information on various topics in science such as robots or the Space Shuttle. They have an

edition on light stock paper and a more expensive version on heavy stock paper. A subscription includes 8 issues a year from September to May. December and January are bimonthly. **Grades K through 4**.

SuperScience

Scholastic Inc.
Post Office Box 3710
Jefferson City, Missouri 65101
800-631-1586

SuperScience makes science fun. This activity-based science magazine is published monthly and is available in two versions. *SuperScience Red* is for **grades 1 through 3** and *SuperScience Blue* is for **grades 4 through 6**. They also have a teachers edition that includes task cards and displays.

Cricket

The Cricket Magazine Group
Box 7434
Red Oak, Iowa 51591-2434
800-827-0227
http://www.musemag.com

This magazine is designed for children **ages 9 to 14**. It offers stories, folk tales, history, science, sports and crafts. A one year subscription includes 12 issues. Go to the web site for more information.

Boy's Life

Boy's Life, Dept. 202   or   1325 W. Walnut Hill
                                Lane
P.O. Box 152079   P.O. Box 152079
Irving, Texas 75015-9963   Irving, TX 75015-2079
214-580-2088

This magazine is published by the Boy Scouts of America. Members of the Boy Scouts of America can receive special rates through local offices. Published monthly.

Muse

Box 7468
Red Oak, Iowa 51591-2468
800-827-0227
http://www.musemag.com

Muse from the publishers of Cricket and Smithsonian magazine is published bimonthly and covers everything from dinosaurs to space travel. **Ages 6 to 14** will enjoy reading about new technologies, music, art, rain forests and more. It encourages kids to write and send in their stories. Go to the web site to see a sample issue and more information.

The earth and ocean seem
To sleeps in one another's arms, and dream
Of waves, flowers, clouds, woods, rocks, and all that we
Read in their smiles and call reality.
—Percy Bysshe Shelley, Epipsychidion

Cobblestone Publishing, Inc.

7 School Street

Peterborough, New Hampshire 03458

800-821-0115

603-924-7209

http://www.cobblestonepub.com

Cobblestone Publishing offers a wide variety of magazines. Each magazine from Cobblestone Publishing can be purchased for the individual and they offer a special rate for classroom subscriptions. Cobblestone also publishes a line of books such as *Mind-Boggling Astronomy* by Steven R. Wills. This is a book with a sense of humor that covers the spectrum of astronomy and space from the ancient skywatchers to the modern thoughts of Einstein and Hawking. The following titles are Cobblestone magazines:

Calliope features world history themes with major articles including maps, timelines, illustrations, pictures of art from major museums and activities. They offer individual or classroom subscriptions for **grades 4 through 9**.

FACES is published in cooperation with the American Museum of Natural History and uses articles, activities, folktales and legends to introduce diverse cultures to grades 4 through 9. Articles often cover a cultures clothing, games, traditions and even recipes of local foods.

Cobblestone features historically accurate articles covering American History. It includes historic photographs, illustrations, primary documents, maps, activities and contests to appeal to young readers in grades 4 through 9.

ODYSSEY is the science magazine that features articles related to astronomy, interviews with scientists, photographs, illustrations, classroom and home activities, recommendations on books to read, places to visit, films to watch and frequent contests for grades 4 through 9. Readers can submit their artwork and connect online with kids and classrooms around the globe.

Dolphin Log

The Cousteau Society
870 Greenbrier Circle Suite 402
Chesapeake, Virginia 23320
800-441-4395

Dolphin Log isn't just about dolphins. This magazine for children **ages 7 to 12** features articles and photos of the ocean and the environment. Children will discover facts about creatures of the land and sea. The Cousteau Society publishes six issues a year.

National Geographic World

Post Office Box 2330
Washington DC 20013-2330
800-647-5463

This magazine visits different areas of the world and features maps, photos, projects and articles for **ages 8 to 12**. The National Geographic Society also has catalogs of products. Call and ask for a member catalog or a catalog of maps, globes and atlases. They have mural maps that are 110" x 76".

Clavier's Piano Explorer
200 Northfield Road
Northfield, Illinois 60093
847-446-8550

> *Piano Explorer* is a great magazine for children **ages 8 to 12**. Each issue features a composer of the month and is filled with word search puzzles, articles and compositions. It encourages young musicians to submit their own compositions and is published monthly except June and August.

New Moon
Post Office Box 3587
Duluth, Minnesota 55803-3587
218-728-5507
800-381-4743
Fax 218-728-0314
http://www.newmoon.org/

> *New Moon* is a magazine edited by girls for girls **ages 8 to 14**. It is educational and focuses on a wide range of topics. Readers are encouraged to send in poetry, letters and stories.

Time For Kids
800-777-8600
http://pathfinder.com/TFK/index.html

> *Time For Kids* is a weekly periodical of current events in an understandable format for children in

grades 4 through 6. They have special rates for classrooms which includes a teacher's guide and they are also introducing a teen edition for **grades 7 through 9.**

WonderScience

American Chemical Society
Post Office Box 3337
Columbus, Ohio 43210
800-333-9511
Fax 614-447-3671

Each issue of *WonderScience* focuses on one topic such as optical illusions and presents activities, materials lists and detailed instructions for parents and children to experiment with together.

Scholastic Math Magazine

2931 East McCarty Street
Post Office Box 3710
Jefferson City, Missouri 65102-3710
800-631-1586

This magazine is great for students in **7th through 9th grade** interested in math. It features projects, equations and articles. It makes math fun and exciting by hosting popular stars.

School Mates

United States Chess Federation
186 Route 9W
New Windsor, New York 12553

> *School Mates* is published by the U.S. Chess Federation and includes tips and hints on chess strategy and features articles on junior chess players. This magazine is designed for chess enthusiasts.

Soccer Jr.

Post Office Box 420442
Palm Coast, Florida 32142-9744
800-829-5382

> *Soccer Jr.* has articles featuring top soccer players, quizzes, and tips to improve the skills of readers **ages 8 to 16**. A subscription includes 6 issues a year.

Sports Illustrated for Kids

Post Office Box 830606
Birmingham, Alabama 35282-9487
800-323-1422
http://www.sikids.com

> This is a monthly magazine for boys and girls **ages 8 to 14** who are sports enthusiasts. A subscription includes 12 monthly issues and a Sports Illustrated for Kids Sports Parent's edition which is published bi-annually.

Stone Soup

Post Office Box 83
Santa Cruz, California 95063
800-447-4569
http://www.stonesoup.com

This magazine is published by the Children's Art Foundation and features stories and artwork by young readers. The magazine is printed on quality stock paper and is an excellent way to promote creativity.

Tomorrow's Morning

160 North Thurston Avenue
Los Angeles, California 90049
800-292-7313
310-440-2778
http://morning.com

Tomorrow's Morning is a newspaper for children **ages 8 to 14**. Designed for groups, the paper introduces students to international, national, arts, book, finance, sports and nature news. It is printed on high quality paper and includes color photos and illustrations. The paper is delivered weekly to the home or classroom.

Plays Drama Magazine for Young People

120 Boylston St.
Boston, Massachusetts 02116-4615

This magazine features plays only. They do not feature articles. It is great for a group of actors who want to practice their skills or even give a performance. **Junior high to high school.**

Nineteenth Avenue

The Humphrey Forum

612-624-5799

> *Nineteenth Avenue* is a newspaper for **ages 12 to 18**. It focuses on current issues such as human rights, curfews and smoking. It promotes community service and motivates students to be active citizens.

Exploring Magazine

Subscription Dept.

3601 Lyon St.

San Francisco, California 94123

415-561-0393

> This is a magazine of science, art and human perception for **ages 13 and up**. Each issue covers a topic in depth, such as, memory, hands, sports and patterns. Teachers can explore new ideas for their lesson plans. It is published quarterly by the Exploratorium, a science and discovery museum.

The Wall Street Journal Classroom Edition

800-544-0522

> This edition is a full color monthly paper for **secondary school students**. It includes articles from the daily *Wall Street Journal* and links the news with students' lives. It also includes a monthly teacher's

guide filled with lesson plans, activities and colorful posters. A single subscription includes 9 issues from September through May. They offer special rates for classrooms.

Biography Today

Omnigraphics, Inc.
ATTN: Order Dept.
Penobscot Building
Detroit, Michigan 48226

> *Biography Today* profiles people of different interests from Jim Lovell, Selena and Debbi Fields. Each issue features people who are prominent in today's world. A subscription includes 3 issues a year. They also have a series devoted to artists, scientists, sports and world leaders.

Career World

Weekly Reader Corporation
3001 Cindel Drive
Delran, New Jersey 08370

> *Career World* is published 7 times during the school year from September through May. It is only available in bulk with a minimum of 15 subscriptions to one address so it is appropriate for schools or clubs. The cost is usually under $10.00 per student. It includes tips and articles on finding a career and how to approach SATs and college visits. This magazine is appropriate for **high school juniors and seniors**.

The Concord Review

Post Office Box 661
Concord, Massachusetts 01742
800-331-5007
http://www.tcr.org

> *The Concord Review* raises the standard for excellence in high school history classes. The quarterly journal publishes essays by students of history. The essays are challenging and impressive. They are a great way to teach and motivate students as well as bolster a college application by submitting works for publication.

Current Health 2

245 Long Hill Drive
Middletown, Connecticut 06457
800-446-3355
http://www.weeklyreader.com

> *Current Health 2* is published monthly during the school year beginning in September and ending in May. This award winning magazine focuses on teen health and features articles on current topics such as smoking prevention, drunk driving and fitness. They also answer questions about health-related concerns sent in by readers. There is a minimum of 15 subscriptions to one address and the subscription cost is $8.65 per student .

National Geographic Research

Post Office Box 2330
Washington DC 20013-2330
800-647-5463
202-857-7000

A scientific journal published by the National Geographic Society and written for those with advanced reading and comprehension skills. This magazine features book reviews and articles on the latest research and discoveries. Incredible photos, illustrations and diagrams supplement the research.

Scientific American

415 Madison Avenue
New York, New York 10017
800-333-1199
515-247-7631

Scientific American is published monthly and features articles on the latest scientific inventions and discoveries and how they are put to use in our world. Subjects frequently reported on are ecology, human health, medicine, space and technology. The articles are written for those with advanced reading and comprehension skills. Scientific American also has a catalog of educational products.

Art to Zoo

Smithsonian Institution, MRC-402
Office of Elementary and Secondary Education
Arts and Industries Building
Room 1163
Washington, DC 20560
202-357-2425
Fax 202-357-2116

> Art to Zoo is a free publication for teachers of grades 3 through 6. The publication features exhibit-based lessons and activities focusing on science, social studies and art. Each issue includes a lesson plan, objectives, background information and a list of materials.

Children's Software

720 Kuhlman
Houston, Texas 77024
713-467-8686
http://www.ultra.net/~jlengel/csp/
http://www.ultra.net/~jlengel/kch/

> Children's Software is published by the Children's Software Press and the Department of Computing in Education at Teacher's College, Columbia University. This quarterly newsletter for parents and teachers is a great resource to stay current on software and web sites for children. It includes articles, reviews, special offers and tips on computers for children.

Homeschooling Today

Post Office Box 1425
Melrose, Florida 32666
904-475-3088

> *Homeschooling Today* offers ideas and models for those who educate at home. Issues are filled with activities, study ideas, science articles, product reviews, lessons on literature and art and more.

Parenting for High Potential

National Association for Gifted Children
1707 L Street, NW
Suite 550
Washington, DC 20036
202-785-4268

> *Parenting For High Potential* is a quarterly magazine designed to help parents develop their children's gifts and talents to their fullest potential. Each issue features expert advice columns, software reviews, book reviews, ideas from parents and a pullout section for children. The NAGC has a number of other publications including *Gifted Child Quarterly* which offers research studies and manuscripts on creative insights about giftedness and talent development in context of the home, the school and the wider society.

Parent's Choice

Box 185
Waban, Massachusetts 02168
617-965-5913
Fax 617-965-4516
http://www.ctw.org

> *Parent's Choice* is a non-profit consumer guide to children's media. The information is distributed by the Children's Television Workshop at www.ctw.org. Members of the Parent's Choice Foundation receive press releases and other advance information.

Roeper Review

Post Office Box 329
Bloomfield Hills, Michigan 48303-0329
810-642-1500

> *The Roeper Review* is published by The Roeper School, a non-profit co-educational school in Michigan for gifted students. This quarterly journal covers international developments and controversies of concern to all professionals and parents involved with gifted education. It presents state and national legislation, innovative programs, curriculum trends, books and research affecting the gifted.

Reading is to the mind what exercise is to the body.
–Richard Steele, The Tatler, no. 147

PROGRAMS OFFERED THROUGH MUSEUMS AND ORGANIZATIONS

Children's museums are a great place to let children explore and have a hands-on learning experience. Many classes and workshops offered by museums can fill up and demos may only take place during certain hours. If you are planning on visiting a museum call to find out if they are having any special programs or classes that you may need to sign up for in advance. You may also want to call if you will have a group of eight or more. On crowded days, some museums have to deny access to large groups who have not prescheduled and special rates are sometimes available to large groups of children.

I have only included a portion of the museums that have special programs for children and teens so if you do not find one in your area, visit the Hands-On Science Centers World Wide web site at http://www.cs.cmu.edu/~mwm/sci.html.

The Ann Arbor Hands On Museum

219 E. Huron Street
Ann Arbor, Michigan 48104
313-995-5439

The Ann Arbor Hands On Museum offers Summer Science Camp, Writing Camp, family programs, outreach programs, workshops, classes and more. The camps are for all ages and feature morning classes, evening classes, lunch classes or all day programs. The Family Programs are hosted by a school and include 2 hours of hands-on activities designed for families. The programs offered are Family Astronomy, Family Biology, Family Chemistry, Family Math I & II and Family Physics.

The Art Institute of Chicago

111 South Michigan Avenue
Chicago, Illinois 60603-6110
312-443-3689 or
312-443-3600

The Art Institute of Chicago has a wide range of programs to offer children and adults. The Kraft Education Center features family workshops, guided tours, gallery walks, artist demonstrations, drawing in the galleries, games and activities. Many family workshops take place on the weekend and children can enjoy making special projects or seeing a performance. They have activities designed for grandparents and grandchildren ages 6 and up called The Grand Program.

The School of the Art Institute of Chicago also offers programs for children and adults. They have intergenerational programs which include Art-in-the-Park, Art-in-the-Libraries and year around community based sites. The Early College Program is for high school students who are considering the study of visual and fine arts in higher education. They also offer classes for adults. Adults and high school juniors and seniors may receive college credit for many of the courses.

The Brooklyn Children's Museum

145 Brooklyn Avenue
Brooklyn, New York 11213
718-735-4400

The world's first children's museum has a host of

activities at the museum as well as hands-on activity
books and teacher's guides.

California Academy of Sciences

Golden Gate Park
San Francisco, California 94118-4599
415-221-5100

> The California Academy of Sciences includes an
> aquarium, a natural history museum, a planetarium
> and a discovery room. They offer after-school and
> Saturday classes as well as activity books, kits with
> curriculum guides, lending materials and teacher's
> guides.

Children's Museum Portland

3037 SW Second Avenue
Portland, Oregon 97201
503-823-2227

> The Portland Children's Museum has an outreach
> membership program for low income families. It
> includes free admission for your entire family for six
> months and ten dollars in credits to be used in any of
> the Museum's drop-in Clayshop activities.

The Children's Museum of Rhode Island

58 Walcott Street
Pawtucket, Rhode Island 02860-4111
401-726-2591

> The Children's Museum of Rhode Island offers many
> after school programs and events such as Preschool

Fridays, Make It and Take It, volunteer programs, Pizzazz Performance Series in February and April, and free admission to the Museum the first Sunday of every month. They also have a hands-on traveling exhibit called You Who?! It is designed to travel to schools, shopping centers, fairs and festivals for a fee. It is appropriate for grades K through 8.

The Discovery Center of Idaho
131 Myrtle
Boise, Idaho 83702
208-343-9895

The Discovery Center of Idaho offers classes on the weekend for children. The classes for children ages 6 to 7 cover a variety of subjects such as prisms and rainbows, colored shadows, bubbleology, mirrors and light lab. Children ages 8 to 9 can take classes on optical illusions, lenses and light. The classes involve activities such as building a pinhole camera.

Dolphin Research Center
U.S. Highway at Mile Marker 59
Grassy Key, Florida 33052
305-289-1121

The Dolphin Research Center provides curriculum guidelines, career information on marine mammal science and a week long college accredited undergraduate level program. The program also offers classes for ages 15 to 17.

EQUALS Programs

Lawrence Hall of Science
University of California
Berkeley, California 94720-5200
510-642-1823
Fax 510-643-5757
equals@maillink.berkeley.edu   :email

EQUALS offers three programs, Equals in Mathematics, Sequals and Family Math. EQUALS programs work to increase access and equity in mathematics for traditionally under-represented students such as females, students of color, children from low-income families and those from language minority groups. The programs are for teachers, parents, counselors and administrators and are offered around the world. EQUALS in Mathematics promotes thoughtful approaches to mathematics with good strategies and materials. SEQUALS invites EQUALS alumni back for new mathematics and equity sessions on innovative mathematics curricula and instructional topics.

EQUALS offers a number of publications at reasonable prices. A few are:

EQUALS Investigations is a series covering scatter plots, correlation, cause and effect, linear and exponential growth models, proportional reasoning and distance, measurement of distance and angle, and surface area, volume and scale. Each unit challenges students on an individual and a group level and can be used in bilingual or multilingual classrooms.

Other publications are:

Get It Together: Math problems for groups grades 4 through 12.

Math For Girls: designed to encourage girls' enjoyment of math in levels k through 8.

Teachers' Voices, Teachers' Wisdom: Seven adventurous teachers tell how they help students learn and make discoveries.

Family Math: Families enjoy math activities at home by using simple everyday objects. Grades K through 8. Also available in Spanish, Matematica Para La Familia.

101 Short Problems: A collection of mathematics problems for children in grades 2 through 9. Also available in Spanish, 101 Problemas Cortos.

Assessment Alternatives in Math: Reviews methods to assess students' performances and encourage student self-assessment.

Off and Running: Introduces students to concepts of computer work such as Boolean algebra, default assumptions, and sequence of commands through a story of a 12 year olds summer with Aunt Bebe. Grades 4 through 12.

Spaces: Students learn problem solving skills and different career paths in engineering, science and technology. Grades 4 through 10.

Family Math provides materials to promote family participation in mathematics and ways for families to become involved in their children's mathematics education.

For further information about Family Math contact

the program in a city near you.
A list of cities, states and countries that have Family
Math programs:

Alaska
Fairbanks

Arizona
Tucson

California
Fresno
Los Angeles
Orange County
Riverside County
San Diego
Stockton

Colorado
Denver

Connecticut
Glastonbury

Florida
Miami

Idaho
Boise

Illinois
Chicago
Edwardsville

Indiana
Indianapolis
Muncie

Iowa
Ames

Kansas
Topeka

Louisiana
Donalsonville

Maine
Augusta

Maryland
Rockville

Massachusetts
Pittsfield
Springfield
Worcester

Michigan
Ann Arbor

Minnesota
Minneapolis
Rochester

Nevada
Las Vegas

New Jersey
New Brunswick

New Mexico
Albuquerque
Sante Fe

New York
Albany
Larchmont
New York

North Carolina
Hendersonville
Wilson

North Dakota
Grafton

Ohio	**Texas**	**Canada**
Cleveland	Austin	Toronto, Ontario
Kent	Houston	Vancouver, BC

Oregon	**Vermont**	**Costa Rica**
Portland	Groton	San José
	Waterbury Center	
Pennsylvania		**New Zealand**
Edinboro	**Virginia**	Takapuna Auckland
	Richmond	
Puerto Rico		**South Africa**
San Juan	**Washington DC**	Braamfontein

South Carolina	**Wyoming**	**Sweden**
Columbia	Laramie	S-951 87 Luleä
		S-20045, Malmö
Tennessee	**Australia**	
Knoxville	Broadway New South	**Venezuela**
Memphis	Wales	Maracaibo
	Hawthorne Victoria	

The Imaginarium Science Discovery Center

725 W. 5th Avenue
Anchorage, Alaska 99501
907-276-3179

> The Imaginarium has traveling exhibits and a Camp-In Adventure. They also have an adopt-a-school program with local businesses.

Monterey Bay Aquarium

http://www.mbayaq.org/

> The Monterey Bay Aquarium will take you on a tour of one of the world's richest marine environments. The online gift and bookstore features a wonderful selection of books on creatures such as sea otters, sharks and gray whales.

Museum of Science

Science Park
Boston, Massachusetts 02114-1099
800-729-3300
617-589-0437
Fax 617-589-0474

> This is a children's museum that offers a program called Science by Mail. Science by Mail is a pen pal program with science teachers and children from grades 4 through 9. They participate in projects and share their results with the other children in the program. They also have a class pack option for classrooms.

Museum of Science and History, Jacksonville

1025 Museum Circle
Jacksonville, Florida 32207-9053
904-396-7062

> The Museum of Science and History has a variety of programs that come to you.
> Watt Is Electricity is an award winning program teaching the basics of electricity and electrical safety.

Burning Questions, The Science of Fire stresses safety with topics covering smoke detectors, fire extinguishers, flame retardant clothing and Stop, Drop and Roll.

The Neon Ninjas, Martial Arts, Math and Motion presents mathematics and motion by combining martial arts and black lights.

The Nuts and Bolts of Lightening presentation uses the one million volt Tesla coil to create a workable substitute for lightening bolts.

The Timucuan, Native American Lifeways introduces students to what life was really like for the first inhabitants of Northeast Florida.

Live Animal Outreach takes a close look at predators and answers questions like "Why is a frog's tongue put in backwards?"

Museum of Science and Industry, Chicago

57th Street and Lake Shore Drive
Chicago, Illinois 60637-2093
312-684-1414

The Museum of Science and Industry offers a variety of programs for students and teachers. They have workshops for teachers and school staff members, activity and teacher guides to support the exhibits and the NASA Teacher Resource Center which is a supply of tapes, slides and other materials about the U.S. Space Exploration Program.

Some of their programs for students are:

The role Models and Leaders Project is for high school students traditionally under represented in science, math, business and technology. It is a competitive program in which students apply for participation in their junior year. The selected students are exposed to a variety of careers and are provided with a mentor to inform and support them as they prepare for college.

The New Explorers Series is series of videotapes and activity guides that teach students scientific principle and concepts through hands-on activities and real world connections.

MSI Scholars offers qualified students free admission to the Museum daily after 2 p.m. on school days and daily the rest of the year. The students must be attending elementary or high school within the City of Chicago and must complete the application process.

MSI Science Club meets every other Saturday in Seabury Labs to investigate a wide variety of math and science topics.

MSI Science Club Network consists of science clubs throughout the Chicago area that meet after school or weekends at a hosting school or community center.

Science Fairs and CICI Career Day are held annually.

The Natural History Museum, Los Angeles

900 Exposition Boulevard
Los Angeles, California 90007
213-744-3466
http://www.lam.mus.ca.us

Find a host of educational programs such as classes

for schools, youth and family programs, adult lectures, classes and travel programs, community outreach programs, artifacts for loan, research programs for high school students and volunteer opportunities.

North Carolina Museum of Life and Science

433 Murray Avenue.
Post Office Box 15190
Durham, North Carolina 27704
919-220-5429

The North Carolina Museum of Life and Science has programs for teachers and students including a Museum Discovery Club and Winter and Summer Science Camps.

Public Allies

1151 K Street, NW, Suite 330
Washington, D.C. 20005
202-638-3300

Public Allies introduces young people ages 18 to 30 to public service, team work and a group experience. Participants serve non-profit organizations for a ten month apprenticeship. Call for more information.

San Diego Zoo

2920 Zoo Drive
San Diego, California 92103
619-231-1515

The San Diego Zoo offers classes and traveling

exhibits. They also feature audiovisual materials, live animals for loan, a catalog of materials and curriculum packets on topics such as dinosaurs and rain forests.

Santa Barbara Botanic Garden
1212 Mission Canyon Road
Santa Barbara, California 93105-2199
805-682-4726

> The Botanic garden features curricula for elementary school students. A few of the activity based resource guides are *Happenin' Habitats* for grades 3 through 8 and the *Nature Kit: From Seeds to Sprouts* for grades K through 6. Activity pages are printed in English and Spanish. Call for a flier listing the publications offered.

Sea World
Education Department
1720 South Shores Road
San Diego, California 92109-7995
800-380-3202
619-226-3834
http://www.seaworld.org/

> Schools throughout the western United States may participate in assembly programs and interactive television programs from Sea World via satellite. The marine center also offers materials for the computer and a catalog from the Education Department. The catalog features well priced videos and teacher's guides such as Marine Mathematics.

SOFTWARE

Each year, hundreds of new software titles are introduced so reading reviews is a good way to narrow down the search to finding educational and enjoyable titles for children. All of the titles included in this chapter have been recognized with awards or positive reviews. Most of the companies have demos available at their web site and the ability to order online and ship internationally.

Brøderbund Software

500 Redwood Blvd.
Novato, California 94948
800-521-6263
800-474-8840   educators orders
http://www.broderbund.com

Just a few of the many titles published by Brøderbund are:

James Discovers Math: Children **ages 3 to 6** visit 10 exciting areas in Jame's kitchen while he counts his ingredients.

Kid Pix Studio: Add movement, video, sound effects and music to pictures. **Ages 6 to 9**.

Math Workshop: Children **ages 6 to 10** make connections between music and math, launch rockets, find hidden picture patterns and solve equations all with multiple difficulty levels.

The Amazing Writing Machine: Children **ages 6 to 12** compose storybooks, essays, poems and write letters.

Carmen Sandiego Junior Detective Edition: Children **ages 5 to 8** will apply strategy, memory and matching skills while exploring geography to solve a mystery. This CD-Rom does not require reading.

Where in the World is Carmen Sandiego?: As a detective out to solve a crime, you will tour the world and encounter maps, flags, state essays, regional music, color photos, video clips and panoramic landscapes. **Ages 9 and up**. All of these titles have won honors and awards. Visit the web site to order online.

Corel

Corel Building
1600 Carling Avenue
Ottawa, Ontario
K1Z 8R7   Canada
800-455-3169 USA and Canada
0800-581028 United Kingdom
800-658-850 Australia
+353-1-706-3912 Worldwide
http://www.corel.com

Corel Adventures With Edison: Kids explore electricity, friction and gravity at the wild science arcade. On the mystery tour through the museum children will discover sign language, binary math and more. The Rock and Bach studio allows children to compose and produce their own songs and music videos while experimenting with different music styles. For **ages 7 to 14**.

Corel also features The Complete Shakespeare Collection of 37 plays, 5 poems and 154 sonnets on one CD-ROM.

Creative Wonders

800-543-9778

http://www.cwonders.com/

> Grammar Rock: Children **ages 6 to 10** learn grammar concepts through 19 multi-level activities.

Davidson & Associates

19840 Pioneer Avenue

Torrance, California 90503

800-545-7677

310-793-0600

http://www.davd.com/

> Math Blaster Jr.: Children **ages 4 to 7** will encounter numbers and quantities, addition and subtraction, geometric shapes and colors, number sentences, counting to 20 and more.
>
> Alge-Blaster 3: Covers integers, order of operations, monomials, radical expressions, graphing, systems of equations, polynomials, algebraic fractions, factoring, quadratic equations and word problems. **Ages 12 to adult**.
>
> Math Blaster 2, Secret of the Lost City: Children **ages 8 to 13** will discover whole and negative numbers, decimals, fractions and percentages and more with graphics, speech and sound effects.
>
> Reading Blaster invasion of the Word Snatchers: Children **ages 7 to 10** will learn to distinguish between antonyms and synonyms, spell, apply logic skills to reading, build vocabulary and more.
>
> The Multimedia Workshop: Use the video, writing or paint workshop to create movies, presentations,

stationery and more.

Discovery Channel Multimedia

Discovery Channel Catalog
Two Explore Lane
Post Office Box 788
Florence, Kentucky 41022-0788
800-889-9950
301-986-0444
Fax 606-342-0633
http://www.discovery.com

The discovery channel multimedia has developed a CD-ROM titled Connections. It takes viewers on an adventure through history and inventions. The purpose of the CD-ROM game is to save the universe by uncovering hidden links in history. It features live actors placed in computer generated environments. This is not an educational tutorial but a nice alternative to other games for the computer. Visit the web site to find titles that cover history, inventions and more.

Dorling Kindersley Multimedia

800-467-9580
http://www.dk.com/

My First Amazing World Explorer: Tour the world to find people, animals and landscapes. Click on any of the 44 animated maps and find 400 pop-up fact windows, 15,000 text entries and nearly every word narrated. Hear the call of the howler monkey and watch polar bears hunt for food in the Arctic. It also includes 2 activity books, a poster, a jigsaw puzzle, stickers and postcards for **ages 4 to 9**. Visit the web site to order online, discover more titles and the DK Multimedia's address and phone number in your country.

Edmark Corporation

Post Office Box 97021
Redmond, Washington 98073-9721
800-691-2986
206-556-8484
http://www.edmark.com/

A few of Edmark products are:

Sammy's Science House: Children **ages 3 to 6** learn about plants, animals, minerals, fungi, seasons and weather while participating in activities that involve sorting, sequencing, predicting and constructing.

Bailey's Book House: Children **ages 2 to 5** build literacy skills by exploring the sounds and meanings of letters, words, sentences and rhymes. All directions and written words are spoken.

Millie's Math House: Children **ages 2 to 5** learn to recognize and read numerals, learn shapes and practice addition and subtraction facts.

Mighty Math Number Heroes: Multiplication and division, fractions, 2D geometry and probability for **ages 8 to 12** or 3rd through 6th grade math.

Thinkin' Things Collection 3: Children **ages 7 to 13** make trades with brokers around the world, program a half time show and solve the case of the empty Fripple House. They build problem solving skills such as deductive and inductive reasoning, synthesis and analysis.

The Edutainment Catalog

Post Office. Box 21330
Boulder, Colorado 80308
800-338-3844
http://www.edutainco.com

This is an extensive catalog of educational software for **all ages**. Call to receive a catalog or go online. They also have a Philips Media catalog of products including the Fun With Electronics series.

IBM

11400 Burnet Road
Austin, Texas 78758
800-426-7235 Extension 4777
512-838-9441
http://www.us.pc.ibm.com/multimedia/

Emergency Room is an interactive CD-ROM that enrolls you as a medical student at Legacy Hospital. It is designed for entertainment but packed with information as you work your way up to chief of staff by performing basic medical procedures on virtual patients.

Imagination Pilots Entertainment

800-693-3253
http://www.warneractive.com/index.html

Download a playable demo of Where's Waldo?

Exploring Geography and travel around the globe to 7 continents and 130 countries.

KidSoft

10275 N. De Anza Blvd.
Cupertino, California 95014-2237
800-354-6132
408-255-3434
Fax 408-342-3500
http://www.kidsoft.com/

KidSoft licenses and republishes quality CD-ROMS. They offer titles under $20. Their products wear the Good Housekeeping Seal of Approval.

Early Math: Children **ages 3 to 6** learn about numbers with easy point and click responses that do not require reading.

Compton's Children's Encyclopedia: This encyclopedia set has an idea search feature, interactive atlas, online dictionary and thesaurus and over 8,000 full color and black and white pictures for **ages 8 and up**.

Zootopia: Children **ages 8 and up** travel to the forgotten island, Zootopia, to meet 43 different dancing and talking animals. It also includes a reference library with hundreds of facts about animals.

Kidsoft also carries a series of Eyewitness Encyclopedias.

Knowledge Adventure, Inc.

1311 Grand Central Avenue.

Glendale, California 91201

800-542-4240

818-246-8412

http://www.adventure.com

Knowledge Adventure, Inc. offers educational CD-ROM titles for children. It is one of the few companies that offer a title for toddlers ages 18 months to 3 years. A few titles in their Jumpstart series are:

Jumpstart Toddlers (**18 mo. to 3 yrs.**): Children learn the alphabet, numbers and vocabulary words.

Jumpstart Preschool 1 (**2 to 5 yrs.**): Children learn letters, numbers, shapes and colors, puzzles and games.

Jumpstart Kindergarten (**4 to 6 yrs.**): This title involves letter combinations, pre-reading, solving problems, colors, shapes and sequencing.

Jumpstart First Grade (**5 to 7 yrs.**): Designed to teach geography, science, early math, music and reading comprehension.

Jumpstart Second Grade (**6 to 8 yrs.**): Involves puzzles, writing comprehension, higher math, science, basic grammar, music, U.S. geography and more.

Jumpstart Third Grade (**7 to 9 yrs.**): Involves reading, spelling, math, science, music, art , riddles and scavenger hunts.

Jumpstart Fourth Grade (**8 to 10 yrs.**): Solve a mystery by applying reading, math, science, art, history, spelling, music and more.

The Learning Company

The Learning Company Customer Service
One Athenaeum St.
Cambridge, Massachusetts 02124
800-227-5609
800-852-2255 Educational Sales
Fax 617-494-5898
http://www.learningco.com/

> Reader Rabbit's Interactive Reading Journey is a top selling reading program around the world. **Ages 3 to 6** learn to identify letters, sort them into words and recognize spelling patterns. You can place your order online or call toll-free.
>
> Learn To Speak Series: Teaches Spanish, French and German to **ages 14 to adult**.

MECC

6160 Summit Drive North
Minneapolis, Minnesota 55430
800-227-5609
612-569-1500
http://www.mecc.com/

> Relive history and experience full-motion video, historical landmarks and an interactive virtual adventure with the CD-ROM titled Oregon Trail II for **ages 10 and up**.

Microsoft

800-376-5125

http://www.microsoft.com/catalog/

http://www.microsoft.com/education/

Scholastic's Magic School Bus Explores the Earth: Children **ages 6 to 10** explore 6 different terrains of earth with games, reports, experiments and activities. They help Arnold find the lost pieces of his rock collection while learning about a cavern, geode crystal and a volcano.

Scholastic's Magic School Bus Explores the Age of Dinosaurs: Children **ages 6 to 10** hunt for the lost photos from Ms. Frizzle's journal while traveling from the Triassic to the Jurassic to the Cretaceous eras. It includes games, activities, videos, reports, facts and clickable animations.

Microsoft's Encarta 97 Encyclopedia uses photographs, maps, illustrations, videos and animation to explore and describe complex concepts to **ages 10 and older**. The cost is a very reasonable annual subscription fee. For a tour, 30 day free trial or more information go to:

http://www.encarta.msn.com/LanguageChoice.asp

Philips Media

800-883-3767

http://www.philipsmedia.com

Digital Lab: Children **ages 8 and up** learn the principles of digital electronics from an animated character that guides them through building real-life digital circuits.

Cybercrafts Fun With Electronics: Children **ages 8 and up** discover the principles of electricity by building over 25 exciting projects that are safe and easy to use.

Princeton Review Publishing

800-367-6808
617-272-7232
http://www.review.com/

The Princeton Review has put The Big Book of Colleges, The Guide to the Best 309 Colleges and The Guide to Paying for College on a CD-ROM titled the College Advisor. It includes Netscape navigator and internet access software to enable you to see the Web pages of the schools in which you are interested. It also allows you to input your academic history and interests to receive a list of potential colleges and an academic rating according to your answers. Go to the web site for the address and phone number in your area or country.

School Zone Publishing, Inc.

Grand Haven, Michigan
800-253-0564
http://www.schoolzone.com/

Alphabet Express: Children **ages 3 and up** will enjoy letter matching, hidden words, dot-to-dots, coloring books, songs and more. This CD-ROM won on the 1996 Apple Computer's HIDE Award for "Most Elegant Product" which is the Human Interface Design Excellence award. It also won the gold award from the Educational Training Category Association for Multimedia International. You can download a demo at their web site.

Sierra On-Line

3380 146th Place SE Suite 300
Bellvue, Washington 98007
800-757-7707
206-649-9800
International Customers +1 206-649-9800
http://www.sierra.com/

The Lost Mind of Doctor Brain is a CD-ROM that includes puzzles, logic problems and mazes that will put problem solving skills to the test.

Simon&Schuster Interactive

800-545-7677
http://www.mcp.com/ssi/ssiSite

Richard Scary's How Things Work in Busy Town: Teaches **ages 3 to 6** the importance of working together in a community and learning skills.

Typing Tutor VII: Designed to teach typing to **ages 9 to 12** by Davidson/Simon & Schuster. Davidson/Simon & Schuster also has a series teaching beginner, intermediate and advanced chess training.

Money Town: Teaches children **ages 5 to 9** basic money math, coin recognition and how to save and spend wisely by helping the characters of Green street reopen their town park.

The Davidson/Simon & Schuster titles can also be

found at the Davidson web site.

Smart Games, Inc.

49 Atlantic Avenue

Marblehead, Massachusetts 01945

800-258-0260

617-639-4769

Fax 617-639-4769

http://www.smartgames.com/

Smart Games Challenge 1: **Ages 14 to Adult** can choose to attack hundreds of logic puzzles which involve vocabulary and math. Get ready because these brain teasers are not easy. In the "Traffic" puzzle, the challenge is to see how efficiently you schedule traffic lights at a series of intersections. Word Melt is a challenge invented by Lewis Carroll about 100 years ago. The challenge is to change one word into another by changing one letter at a time, but every step you must spell an actual English word. You can download a free demo for PC only.

Children's Software Revue

44 Main Street

Flemington, New Jersey 08822

908-284-0404

Fax 908-284-0405

http://www.microweb.com/pepsite

This site was developed in response to the needs of parents, educators and children's software publishers. Find the top software picks from Children's Software Revue database, software ratings tips on how to evaluate software and more.

Download.Com

http://www.download.com/

Go to the kids section to find a list of the newest titles, top picks and most popular titles to download and test.

EPIE Institute

103-3 West Montauk Highway

Hampton Bays, New York 11946

516-728-9100

http://www.epie.org/

The Educational Products Information Exchange Institute offers a database of over 3,000 educational software programs. It is available in MS-DOS, Mactintosh and CD-ROM versions. The EPIE is an organization that evaluates educational products including a Curriculum Analysis Services for Educators.

GameSpot

http://www.gamespot.com/

GameSpot reviews around 40 to 60 games each month. It features tips, instructions and downloads. You may be able to find and test educational games through services such as GameSpot and Happy Puppy.

Happy Puppy

http://happypuppy.com

Happy Puppy is a web site devoted to computer game reviews. It features news, hints and tips as well as game demo downloads. Many people rely on Happy Puppy downloads before purchasing a game.

WEB SITES

THE ARTS

Art & Museums

http://www.vol.it/UK/EN/ARTE/

Access museums covering archeology, architecture, design and photography.

Art Serve: Art and Architecture

http://rubens.anu.edu.au/index2.html

Visit museums, classical sites and learn about the history of art and architecture.

ArtsEdge

http://artsedge.kennedy-center.org/artsedge.html

Discover resources for lesson plans, model programs and links for grades K through 8.

Big Ears, The Original Online Ear Trainer

http://www.pageplus.com/~bigears/

The Big Ears Java applet is designed to help one improve their aural recognition skills.

Claude Monet

http://sunsite.unc.edu:80/louvre/paint/auth/monet

This site is the Web Museum's section on Monet. It includes some of the artist's work, a background of the artist and links to other great masters such as Renoir and Manet.

Claude Monet Homepage

http://www.columbia.edu/~jns16/monet_html/monet
.html

> See paintings or read a biography, a formal analysis
> of one of Monet's work, an overview of impression-
> ism and more.

Educational Theatre Association

http://www.etassoc.org/

> The Educational Theatre Association publishes two
> magazines, *Dramatics* and *Teaching Theatre*.

Le Louvre

http://www.louvre.fr/

> See the incredible collection of antiquities, paintings,
> sculptures and more. In French, English, Spanish
> and Portuguese.

Metropolitan Museum of Art

http://www.metmuseum.org/

> Visit the collections, education department or the
> gift shop at one of the largest art museums in the
> world.

Musée d'Orsay

http://www.paris.org/Musees/Orsay/Collections/Painti
ngs

> View the museums incredible collection of paintings
> by masters such as Monet, Renoir and Degas.

Museum of Modern Art, New York

http://www.moma.org/

> The museum's Department of Education offers a variety of programs including internships, volunteer programs and family and school programs.

Music Education

http://www.jumpoint.com/bluesman/

> Discover educational links, articles and lessons relating to music.

The Sistine Chapel

http://www.christusrex.org/www1/sistine/0-Tour.html

> Built between 1475 and 1483, this chapel has some of the most treasured paintings in the world. The ceiling was repainted in 1508 by Michelangelo and the walls were painted by a host of other masters.

St. Peter's Basilica

http://www.christusrex.org/www1/citta/0-Citta.html

> Visit this incredible basilica in the Vatican City and see pictures of the space and sculptures designed by Michelangelo. Available in many languages.

The Vatican Museums

http://www.christusrex.org/www1/vaticano/0-Musei.html

> View 596 images of the galleries of paintings and sculptures including the Gregorian Etruscan and Egyptian Museums. Available in many languages.

Virtual Library Museum Search

www.comlab.ox.ac.uk/archive/other/museums.html
This site will list nearly every museum in the world
that has a web page! Explore by country, exhibition
or visit one of the many recommended tours.

Web Museum

http://sunsite.unc.edu/wm/   or
http://sunsite.unc.edu/louvre
Visit universities, museums and exhibitions all over
the world. Choose from a number of countries or
take a recommended tour.

Whitney Museum of American Art

http://www.echonyc.com/~whitney/
See exhibitions, the permanent collection and links
to their favorite places like the Cooper-Hewitt,
National Design Museum, the Los Angeles County
Museum of Art and more.

*I try to apply colors like words that shape poems,
like notes that shape music. –Joan Miró*

DISABILITY / SPECIAL NEEDS

Ability Online Support Network

919 Alness Street

North York, ON   M3J2J1   Canada

416-650-6207

Fax 416-650-5073

http://www.ablelink.org

> Ability Online is an electronic mail system that connects young people with a disability or chronic illness to disabled and non-disabled peers and mentors.

Different Roads to Learning

http://www.difflearn.com

800-853-1057

Fax 800-317-9146

> This is an online catalog specializing in educational toys for learning challenged children ages 2 to 9.

The Disability Connection by Apple Computer

http://www2.apple.com/disabilty/welcome.html

> Discover Macintosh assistive technology for individuals with disabilities and links to more disability-related web pages.

Down Syndrome WWW Page

http://www.nas.com/downsyn/index.html

> Discover parent matching and support groups, edu-

cational resources, healthcare guidelines, toy catalogs and more.

Dragonfly Toy Company

http://www.dftoys.com/

The Dragonfly Toy Company provides toys, books and adaptive devices for special needs children. Visit their online catalog or find links to other helpful web sites.

Family Education Network

http://www.familyeducation.com

This is a great site that offers activities to learn and share with your children, resources for families of children with disabilities, expert picks on books and software and tips on how to get involved in your child's learning. They also have an educational store online.

Interactive ASL Guide

http://www.disserv.stu.umn.edu/AltForm/

Learn the alphabet in sign language. You can also find an interactive Braille guide and finger spelling quiz.

Jerome & Deborah's Special Education Links

http://www.mts.net/~jgreenco/special.html

This is a great source for links to special education sites including information on dyslexia and gifted youth programs.

Muscular Dystrophy, "A Guide for Parents"

http://www.mda.org.au/mdag1_1.html

> This site provides information on muscular dystrophy, genetic counseling, DNA testing, risk factors, dietary advice, support services and much more.

Our Kids

http://rdz.stjohns.edu/library/support/our-kids

> Our Kids is a web site that serves parents raising children with special needs. They feature reading lists, nutrition tips, newsgroups for specific challenges such as autism, cerebral palsy and down syndrome and links to many resources.

Special Education Exchange

http://www.spedex.com/   or

http://www.spedex.com/main2.htm

> Access research, professional, resources and job listings for educators, parents and students with disabilities.

Students With Intellectual Disabilities

http://www.educ.gov.bc.ca/.specialed/www/sid/
contents.html

> This site is a guide that includes tips, case studies, resources and references for teachers of students with intellectual disabilities.

GEOGRAPHY / MAPS

Adventure Online

http://www.adventureonline.com

This site is a fantastic guide to following explorers on their travels. You can see their latest photos, read their journals and e-mail the adventurers questions.

Boston.com

http://boston.com

Information on the city of Boston including all of its museums.

Cambridge, U.K.

http://www.cam-orl.co.uk/cgi-bin/pangen

Visit Cambridge via the live cam. In English and Italian.

City.Net

http://www.city.net/

Visit any city around the world and learn about travel, entertainment, local business, government and community services. This is the webs most extensive library of local and regional information.

Cultural Map of Greece

http://www.culture.gr/2/21/maps/hellas.html

View a map of Greece and see the sites and monuments.

Gateway to Antarctica

http://www.icair.iac.org.nz/

> This site has won awards for its information on Antarctic research, environment, education, images, science, news, history, treaty and tourism.

The Geologist's Lifetime Field List

http://www.uc.edu/www/geology/geologylist/index.html

> A list of sites that every geologist and interested web surfer should visit. It features images and links.

Geography World

http://members.aol.com/bowermanb/101g.html

> Discover educational media, games and a large selection of links relating to geography.

InfoNation

http://www.un.org/Pubs/CyberSchoolBus/infonation/

> This site is a database of information for the Member States of the United Nations. You can access data on an area's average rain fall, language, economy, population, growth rate, threatened species and more.

Kid's Corner

http://www.ci.oxford.ms.us/group2/kids/

> A list of activities and features for kids of Oxford, Mississippi.

Lonely Planet

http://www.lonelyplanet.com

A travel guide with phrase books, maps and photos for high school level and up. Virtually travel all over the world.

Map Quest

http://www.mapquest.com

This is an interactive street guide to anywhere in the world. Access maps of Rome, Cairo or Beijing.

National Geographic Online

http://www.nationalgeographic.com

This web site will take you around the world via their amazing images. You will also discover information on the National Geographic Society's line of software.

Paris

http://www.paris.org/

Visit Paris and all of its sites.

You can also visit the following sites of Paris directly:

http://www.paris.org/Monuments

The monuments of Paris

http://www.paris.org/Musees/

http://www.paris.org/Expos/

The museums and exhibitions of Paris

St. Petersburg Pictures Gallery

http://www.spb.su/pictures/index.html

> This is a short visit to St. Petersburg, Russia. View a few pictures of St. Petersburg during the day and night.

Stockholm, Sweden

http://www.ausys.se/weather/weather.exe?medium+eng

> A live view of Stockholm plus an animation of the weather.

UK Active Map

http://www.uktravel.com/ukmap.html

> Click on different locations on the map of the UK to see pictures and information about a city.

United Nations

http://www.un.org

> Find out about UN news, Global Issues, Overview, Photos, Conferences and what is New on the Web.

U.S. Census Bureau

http://www.census.gov

> Pick a location in the U.S. and find its economic profile, population and location.

U.S. Gazetteer

http://www.census.gov/cgi-bin/gazetteer

> Link to U.S. Gazetteer place and zip code files. Enter

a location and it will give you the population, location, zip codes, map and census tables.

U.S.A. CityLink

http://usacitylink.com//
> A list of web sites featuring U.S. cities and states.

Virtual Tourist

http://www.vtourist.com/
> This award winning site is a map based directory of all the servers in the world.

White House

http://www.whitehouse.gov
> Visit the virtual library, briefing room, history and tours or send the President email.

White House Kids Version

http://www.whitehouse.gov/WH/kids/html/home.html
> Learn about the history and location or write the President.

Yosemite National Park

http://www.nps.gov/yose/yo_visit.htm
> View wonderful images of the parks spectacular waterfalls and sites. Check for the latest news, weather or traffic and find programs for educators and internships for college students.

HISTORY

A&E

http://www.aetv.com

This is the site for the television program A&E Biography. It features quizzes, study guides and the week's program schedule.

All American Quiz

http://thok.let.rug.nl/~epu/usmaze/index.htm

Take the All American Quiz and test your knowledge of American History, flags and geography.

The History Channel

http://www.historychannel.com

The History Channel has an archive of famous speeches that can be heard online. You will also discover exhibits, games and over 1,000 video titles that can be purchased from the site.

Israel Museum

http://www.imj.org.il/

Take the museum tour and see the building that holds ancient artifacts such as the Dead Sea Scrolls and the Isaiah Scroll. Sections are also available in Hebrew.

Roman Open Air Museum

http://www.dhm.de/museen/stein/stein_e.html

Visit a Roman villa dating back to the 1st to 3rd Century A.D. In English and German.

Smithsonian Institution

http://www.si.edu

Explore the categories of places, people, activities, perspectives, resources and products. Go to the list of events and activities to see a list of current exhibitions covering the arts, sciences and history.

Splendors of Ancient Egypt

http://www.sptimes.com/Egypt/default.html

Enjoy this online tour of Ancient Egypt and also find a gallery of photographs, Egyptian facts and a study guide on the lives and lands of the Ancients.

Teylers Museum

http://www.teylersmuseum.nl

This museum in the Netherlands is the first virtual museum in the country. See coins, paintings, fossils, minerals and much more. Available in English, Dutch, French and German.

Treasures of the Czars

http://www.sptimes.com/Treasures

The Moscow Kremlin Museums own this exhibit put on-line by the Florida International Museum. Go to the Czar timeline or take a museum tour.

HOUSEHOLD HEALTH AND SAFETY

American Heart Association

http://www.amhrt.org/ahawho.htm

> Did you know taking antioxidant vitamins may reduce cardiovascular disease? Find out more at this educational site. The American Heart Association is a not-for-profit organization dedicated to fighting cardiovascular diseases, the United States' No. 1 killer. Go online to find your local American Heart Association office or call 800-242-8721.

American Psychological Association

http://www.apa.org/

> Find out more about the American Psychological Association, its Help Center or details about a career in psychology.

Centers For Disease Control and Prevention

http://www.cdc.gov/

> Access important health information including publications, products and public health training.

Child Safety Forum

http://www.xmission.com/~gastown/safe/safe2.htm

> This site is a child safety store with security gates, stove guards, corner cushions and much more.

Children's Nutrition Research Center

http://www.bcm.tmc.edu/cnrc

> Read the latest issue of the Nutrition and Your Child newsletter.

Consumer Information Center

http://www.pueblo.gsa.gov/

> They have a catalog of federal publications focusing on numerous subjects including health.

Department of Health and Human Services

http://www.os.dhhs.gov/

> Major public service announcements, current press releases and what's new in the area of health and human services are just a few of the categories on this site.

FinAid, The Financial Aid Information Page

http://www.finaid.com/

> This is the site to search for financial aid programs, college planning, exchange programs, grants, contests and more. Go to the FastWEB section to search a database of over 180,000 private sector scholarships, fellowships, grants and loans or call 800-4-FED-AID.

First Aid Online

http://www.prairienet.org/~autumn/firstaid/

> Find a list of common first aid problems such as poisoning, bites, burns, bruising, fractures and more.

Food and Drug Administration

http://www.fda.gov

Click on the food icon to access materials for educators. This site provides a series of lessons that are designed to help students understand food risks.

Food and Nutrition Information Center

http://www.nal.usda.gov/fnic

Discover dietary guidelines, publications and a food guide pyramid.

healthfinder

http://www.healthfinder.gov/

Healthfinder supplies consumer health information such as self-help groups, non-profit organizations and online publications that will help you make better health choices for you and your family.

International Food Information Council

http://ificinfo.health.org

This site is a great resource for information on food safety and nutrition including publications and resources for educators.

MedWeb

http://www.gen.emory.edu/MEDWEB/medweb.html

Search the country, region or keyword index to reference over 8,000 biomedical links for an answer to your medical question.

National Institutes for Allergies & Infectious Disease

http://www.niaid.nih.gov/

> Access research activities and news in the area of allergies and infectious disease.

National Safe Kids Campaign Homepage

http://www.bixler.com/nskc/nsafekmm2.html

> Does every member of your family know what to do in case of a fire? This site is a great place to learn about family safety. You will find information on residential fire safety, water safety, passenger safety, poison prevention, emergency information and more.

Safe 'N Sound Kids

Post Office Box 100-605
Brooklyn, New York 11210-0605
888-252-2229
718-252-2229
Fax 718-258-4217
http://www.safensoundkids.com

> This is an online catalog with over 300 child safety products. You will also find a list of children's product recalls, safety tips, links and more.

Youth Info

http://youth.os.dhhs.gov

> Discover the latest information about America's adolescents including a profile of America's youth, resources for parents and speeches on youth topics.

LITERATURE

Aesop's Fables

gopher://spinaltap.micro.umn.edu/11/Ebooks/By%20
Title/aesop

> An enormous list of Aesop's fables. Choose the ones
> you would like to read.

Children's Literature Awards Lists

http://www.ucalgary.ca/~dkbrown/awards.html

> This site is the most comprehensive guide to
> English-language children's book awards on the
> internet. Find out what books have received the
> Caldecott Medal, the Hans Christian Andersen
> Medal, the Young Reader's Choice Award and more.

The Children's Literature Web Guide

http://www.ucalgary.ca/~dkbrown/index.html

> This site is a great source for children's bestseller
> lists, movies and television based on children's
> books and more. It is a resource for parents, teach-
> ers, storytellers, writers and illustrators. Go to the
> Classics For Young People and find a list of books on
> the net like Treasure Island, The Wonderful Wizard
> of Oz and Alice's Adventures in Wonderland.

Complete Works of William Shakespeare

http://the-tech.mit.edu/Shakespeare/

Find works of William Shakespeare organized in a table under the categories Comedy, History, Tragedy and Poetry. You will also find Shakespeare resources on the internet, a chronological and alphabetical listing of plays and Bartlett's familiar Shakespearean quotations.

Gopher List of Ebooks

gopher://spinaltap.micro.umn.edu/11

At this gopher site you can find out what the weather is in a particular area of the country. You can also find great books online such as Peter Pan, Moby Dick, Aladdin and the Wonderful Lamp and more.

Imagine: Opportunities and Resources for Academically Talented Youth

http://jhunix.hcf.jhu.edu/~setmentr/imagine.html

A periodical for precollege students who want to take control of their learning. It offers information, insights and counseling to young motivated readers. It requires a paid subscription.

KidPub

http://www.kidpub.org/kidpub/

KidPub offers stories and a list of KidPub schools. Now you can publish stories on the web. You can also find an internet pen pal.

Listening Libraries Hot Link Picks

http://kiwi.futuris.net/listlib/links.html

> This site gives access to a list of bestselling children's books, children's literature web guide and more.

Read Along

http://www.ed.gov/pubs/parents/Reading/ReadAlong.html

> Ideas and activities for parents to make the most of read along time with their children.

Reading is Fundamental

http://www.si.edu/organiza/affil/rif/start.htm

> Activities to awaken and nurture a child's desire to read, publications for parents, parental community involvement and books for children.

Reading Rainbow

http://www.pbs.org/readingrainbow/index.html

> Reading Rainbow sells products and programs to encourage children to read books. Find a list of books and an activity to accompany each book. The direct address to the list is:
> http://www.pbs.org/readingrainbow/rrlist.html

Tales of Wonder

http://itpubs.ucdavis.edu/richard/tales/

> This award winning site offers numerous folk and fairy tales from around the world listed by country.

A word a Day

http://www.wordsmith.org/awad/index.html

Learn a new word every day.

MAGAZINES ONLINE

ION Science

http://www.injersey.com/Media/IonSci/

A monthly magazine on the "latest news and trends in science and nature". Professional science writers and artists explain complex topics and how they affect our lives.

Little Planet Times

http://www.littleplanet.com/

An online magazine designed for kids ages 5 to 10. This site also includes an adult and teacher section and a Pre-K class book.

Lonely Planet

http://www.lonelyplanet.com

A travel guide with phrase books, maps and photos for high school level and up. Virtually travel all over the world.

MidLink Magazine

http://longwood.cs.ucf.edu/~MidLink/

This is an award winning E-zine for 10 to 15 year olds.

Read articles and stories and find lists of on going projects.

National Geographic Online

http://www.nationalgeographic.com
This online magazine will take you on an incredible trek all over the world.

Planet Science

http://www.newscientist.com/
This an online magazine that requires a free registration but non-registered visitors can take a tour.

Popular Science

http://www.popsci.com
Keep up with the latest science news on automobiles, computers, electronics and home tech.

Sports Illustrated for Kids

http://www.sikids.com
The online version of the sports magazine for boys and girls, ages 8 to 14. It features quizzes, interviews with sports heroes, photos and comics.

Time Magazine for Kids

http://pathfinder.com/TFK/index.html
Time For Kids features articles, graphics and facts that teach current events.

MATH

Algebra, Mathematics, Geometry...

http://www.ida.net/users/marie/ed/math.htm
> This site list resources and links involving mathematics, algebra, geometry, calculus and statistics.

The Big Puzzle Archive

http://ftp.cs.ruu.nl/pub/NEWS.ANSWERS/puzzles
/archive
> Find word puzzles on arithmetic, geometry, physics, logic, language, trivia and more.

Geometry Forum Online

http://forum.swarthmore.edu/~steve/index.html
> Complex search of math resources and other subjects and links to projects for students and teachers on the internet.

KCET Mathline

http://www.kcet.org/education/interservice/ml2.htm
> PBS Mathline is public televisions goal to provide online educational services for teachers of mathematics grades K through 8.

Math and Science Gateway

http://www.tc.cornell.edu/Edu/MathSciGateway
> Award winning educational resources on the net and links to museums, field trips and more for educators

and students in grades 9 through 12.

Math Forum

http://forum.swarthmore.edu

The Math Forum includes a student center, a teacher's place, a research division, math resources and education and a division for parents and citizens. Educators will find classroom materials, activities, projects, software, workshops and more.

MathMagic

http://forum.swarthmore.edu/mathmagic/

Problem solving strategies and communication skills for students K through 12. Internet teams discuss solution strategies to a problem.

Math League Help

http://www.mathleague.com/help/help.htm

This is a help site for 4th through 8th grade math students. It covers whole numbers, fractions, geometry, integers, ratio and proportion and more.

Mega Math

http://www.c3.lanl.gov/mega-math/welcome.html

A great way to bring math ideas to the elementary classroom.

PARENT / TEACHER

Alphabet Superhighway

http://www.ash.udel.edu/ash/

Explore resources for parents, teachers and students such as ideas and materials for reports. The site's Cyberzine publishes articles by upper elementary and high school students.

AskERIC

http://ericir.sunsite.syr.edu/

This site is a valuable resource for educators in and out of the classroom. It gives access to a wealth of curriculum materials, research and an opportunity to ask researchers questions.

Children's Television Workshop

http://www.ctw.org/

This is the official online home of Sesame Street. Children can read an interactive storybook or print coloring pages. Parents can find articles on children's health issues, advice columns and the Parent's Guide database.

Classroom Connect

http://www.classroom.net/

A magazine offering conference listings, products, resources and web sites for teachers.

CNN Classroom Guide

gopher://nysernet.org:3000/11/Academic%20Wings/S
ocial%20Studies/CNN%20newsroom%20
classroom%20guide

>This is a gopher menu of classroom guides to daily news and questions to stimulate class discussion.

College Board

http://www.collegeboard.com

>This site for the college bound features information on test dates, test writing skills, financial aid, scholarships, internships, careers and colleges.

CollegeEdge

http://www.collegeedge.com

>CollegeEdge offers advice on careers, colleges, scholarships, majors, financial aid and an online application system.

Common Sense Parenting

http://www.parenting.org

>Check out the Parent's Resource Library, Helpline and Newsletter. This site by Boys Town U.S.A. gives advice to parents of children and teens.

Creative Classroom

http://www.creativeclassroom.org

>The Children's Television Workshop has published this activity magazine to give elementary K through 6th grade teachers creative teaching material. One

subscription includes 6 issues throughout the school year. The web site has more information and fun project ideas.

Discovery Channel School

http://school.discovery.com/

Find a list of upcoming specials, free worksheets, activities and other classroom resources. Great links to pages relating to educating others.

Dr. Toy

http://www.drtoy.com

Search Dr. Toy's database of 100 best children's products and best classic toys.

EdWeb Technology and School Reform

http://edweb.gsn.org/

This site features an educational resource guide, child safety on the information highway and more.

EINet Galaxy Educational Hotlist

http://galaxy.einet.net/galaxy/Social-Sciences/Education.html

Numerous educational links, non-profit organizations, government organizations, collections and events for parents and educators.

Family.com

http://www.family.com/

This site features a guide to events in your home

town and articles on food, health, travel, education and activities. You can also find "365 TV-Free Activities To Do With Your Child" at http://www.family.com/Categories/Activities/

Family Education Network

http://www.familyeducation.com/

This is a great site that offers activities to learn and share with your children, resources for families of children with disabilities, expert picks on books and software and tips on how to get involved in your child's learning.

Family Internet

http://www.familyinternet.com/

Information on parenting, family health, pets, travel, finance, education and more. Ask questions regarding computer problems or visit the reference and resource links for teachers. A great part of this site is Scholastic Place located under education. Scholastic offers book clubs, sponsored programs, K through 8 core and supplemental programs, web links and literacy activities for students.

Family Resource Online

http://www.familyresource.com/

Family Resource Online offers advice, articles, software reviews and links for families. Some of the topics covered are divorce, drug abuse, education, family health and more.

Family Web

http://www.familyweb.com

> The goal of this site is "to provide an informative place for families to gather from around the world".

IAAY - The study of exceptional talent

http://www.jhu.edu:80/~gifted/

> This is the Institute for the Academic Advancement of Youth. Find program opportunities and information about academic advancement.

Intercultural E-Mail Classroom Connections

http://www.stolaf.edu/network/iecc

> This site is devoted to helping teachers and classes link with partners in other countries and cultures. St. Olaf College provides a mailing list for e-mail pen-pal and project exchanges.

Internet for Kids

http://www.internet-for-kids.com/

> Teach your baby how to use the internet. Visit the squirrel cam, the playground for 7 and under and what's new in science.

K-12 Teacher Tool Box

http://www.trc.org/toolbox.htm

> A comprehensive list of resources covering numerous subjects ranging from theater to special education.

K-12 Servers

http://www.tenet.edu/education/main.html
> Resources for K through 12 educators and lists K through 12 servers by state or outside the United States.

KCET

http://www.kcet.org
> The KCET Public Television site features resources for parents, teachers and kids as well as previews of current informative programming.

The Kids on the Web

http://www.zen.org/~brendan/kids.html
> Search educational sites, books, safety on the net and more.

KidSource Online

http://www.kidsource.com
> KidSource offers great information on product news, newborns, toddlers, preschoolers, K through 12 education, health, recreation, forums, parenting, computing EDGE, organizations, guide to the best software, links to organizations and more.

The Mommy Times

http://www.mommytimes.com
> The Mommy Times reports information on recalls, children's media and advice for mothers from mothers.

Library Services For Preschoolers

http://www.ed.gov/pubs/parents/Library/Services.htm
l

> Learn about library programs for infants to school-
> aged children. This site also features tips on how to
> introduce the library experience to a child.

Montessori For Moms

http://www.primenet.com/~gojess/mfm/mfmhome.ht
m

> A collection of lesson plans for home schooling using
> the Montessori teaching method. Uncover a wide
> variety of learning activities for children ages 2
> through 5. The lesson plans involve sensorial devel-
> opment, practical life experiences, beginning reading
> and beginning math.

Mr. Roger's Neighborhood

http://www.pbs.org:80/rogers/

> Go to the Plan and Play activities for ideas on pro-
> jects for kids.

OnlineClass

http://www.usinternet.com/onlineclass

> K through 12 teachers will find programming materi-
> als and opportunities to involve students in global
> classrooms that interactively explore the world.

ParenthoodWeb

http://www.parenthoodweb.com/

A multitude of information about raising children for parents and prospective parents. Discover articles, reviews on products and a section to ask the pros.

Parents and Children Together Online

http://www.indiana.edu/~eric_rec/fl/pcto/menu.html

An online magazine that has features for children listed by grades, book reviews, articles on issues related to children's reading and writing, brochures and stories to be read aloud. The site's goal is to promote family literacy.

Parents Place

http://www.parentsplace.com

A parenting resource on the web for shopping, special chat topics, recipes, book and software reviews and information about children of all ages including teens.

Parent Soup

http://www.parentsoup.com

A parenting resource that requires a free membership for many of its services but non-members can browse too. Parent Soup offers information in all areas of child raising. They also provide discussion groups for parents to ask professionals questions and talk to other parents who may have similar experiences or questions.

Plugged In

http://www.pluggedin.org/

This non-profit group is dedicated to connecting the technological opportunities with the low income area of East Palo Alto, California.

Smithsonian Office of Elementary and Secondary Education

http://educate.si.edu/

This site features curriculum materials, teacher resources, teacher development, electronic services, school partnerships and student internships for high school seniors.

The Stuttering Homepage

http://www.mankato.msus.edu/dept/comdis/kuster/st utter.html#home-page

This site provides information about stuttering, therapy, newsletters, research, fluency related disorders and more.

The Teachers Network

http://www.teachnet.org/

This is a nonprofit organization for teachers. The site features resources such as *The Teachers Guide to Cyberspace*, a database of teacher projects and hands-on curriculum projects.

Teaching and Learning on the Web

http://www.mcli.dist.maricopa.edu/tl/

Pick a subject from a list of categories and this site will search their database for web sites related to that subject on the internet. The database of sites is used to present ideas on how the web is being used as a medium for learning.

Technology and Learning Magazine

http://www.techlearning.com/

This is a publication for technology-using educators and parents. You can find software reviews, a hotlist of lesson plan sources, libraries and museums, sources for online projects and more.

Totware

http://www.het.brown.edu/people/mende/totware.ht ml

Shareware and freeware that fall under the subjects of nature, painting, letters and numbers and more. This is a great site to find inexpensive and free software for young children.

U.S. Department of Education Publications for Parents

http://www.ed.gov/pubs/parents.html

This is a fantastic site to find information benefiting children and teens. The site features the publications Helping Your Child series such as Helping Your Child Learn Math and Helping Your Child Improve in

Test Taking. This site also offers a link to ERIC Parent Brochures regarding parent's concerns about their child's education. Some other publications include Preparing Your Child For College and tips on financial aid programs and home learning activities.

Web66 A K12 World Wide Web Project

http://web66.coled.umn.edu/

This site has won awards for its information on step by step instructions to set up a server and a construction set and more.

www.4kids.org

http://www.4kids.org

Visit this site to see if a newspaper in your area features the www.4kids.org article. This weekly column lists safe, fun and educational sites for children to visit on the web. Go to the web site to find back issue and links.

REFERENCE

Bartlett's Quotations

http://www.columbia.edu/acis/bartleby/bartlett/

Are you looking for a quotation from a passage, phrase or proverb? Search for a quotation by subject or by author.

C-SPAN

http://www.c-span.org

> Learn about congress and the top stories covering the U.S. policymakers. Link to C-SPAN in the Classroom to access lesson plans.

Dictionary.com

http://dictionary.com

> A reference resource with links to sites such as Bartlett's Quotations and Webster Dictionary.

Free Internet Encyclopedia

http://clever.net/cam/encyclopedia.html

> Encyclopedia of information on the internet. Parental guidance for children under 18. Award winning but has not been filtered for the use of young web surfers.

Journal Graphics

http://www.tv-radio.com/

> News from CNN, ABC, PBS and NPR. Topic lists by subject or alphabetically. High School level and older.

Knowledge Adventure Encyclopedia

http://www.adventure.com/encyclopedia

> Use the search command or browse from a list of subjects ranging from aviation to undersea life.

Roget's Thesaurus

http://www.thesaurus.com

> Enter a keyword and press return to start a search.

Webster Dictionary

http://www.m-w.com/netdict.htm

> This site also features a Word Game of the Day and a Language Info Zone which links to interactive vocabulary quizzes.

LIBRARIES

CIC Electronic Journals Collection

http://ejournals.cic.net/

> The CIC electronic journals collection is the place to look for electronic magazines and journals.

Electronic Library

http://www.elibrary.com

> The electronic library is a subscription based site that gives members access to newspapers, magazines, maps, books, TV and radio transcripts and more.

Global Electronic Library

gopher://marvel.loc.gov:70/11/global

> A gopher menu of a wide range of subjects from mathematics to sports and recreation.

Internet Public Library

http://www.ipl.org

> Discover different sections for reference, youth, teen and more. Find an internet newsletter for kids and explore math and science or ask authors and illustrators questions.

Kids Web

http://www.npac.syr.edu/textbook/kidsweb/

> This world wide web digital library for school kids is a great source of information organized by subject.

Library of Congress

http://www.loc.gov/

> The subject categories are people, places, time, topics, events and educator. The library of congress is great for educators who want to look at lesson plans and professional related sights at the learning page.

NCSU Webbed Library

http://dewey.lib.ncsu.edu/

> Access to encyclopedias, dictionaries and subject related internet resources.

The WWW Virtual Library

http://vlib.stanford.edu/Overview.html

> The WWW Virtual Library offers information and links organized under an extensive list subjects.

The WWW Virtual Library Education Search

http://www.csu.edu.au/education/library.html

Educational resources listed alphabetically, by grade, country or type of site.

SCIENCE

Bill Nye, The Science Guy Home Page

http://nyelabs.kcts.org/

Find out what the demo of the day is or if you are looking for a good book check out the books of science list.

Dan's Wild Wild Weather Page

http://www.whnt19.com/kidwx

Kids can learn about clouds, pressure, humidity, tornadoes, hurricanes and much more.

Exploratorium

http://www.exploratorium.edu

A world of information from the Teacher's Institute to What's New In The World and the Digital Library. Go to the Learning Studio to see exhibits and hands on science like virtually dissecting a cow's eye.

Field Museum of Natural History Exhibits

http://www.fmnh.org./

> This is the home page of the Field Museum of Natural History in Chicago, Illinois. Discover online exhibits and teacher's guides at http://www.fmnh.org./exhibits/exhibits.htm

Florida Museum of Natural History

http://www.flmnh.ufl.edu

> Visit the online exhibits at the Virtual Museum and find out what's new on the museum web.

Franklin Institute of Virtual Science Museum

http://sln.fi.edu/

> This site has so much to explore. Go to the online exhibits, educational hotlists, online magazine, "InQuiry Almanac", find units of study to support your science curriculum or learn basic skills to explore the web.

Girls For Science

http://www.hopper.com/scigirl.html

> Girls work together on the WWW to complete a scavenger hunt with questions such as what are the five elements of African Art? or what is the main use of the Poison Arrow Frog?

Hands-On Science Centers World Wide

http://www.cs.cmu.edu/~mwm/sci.html

> Visit an exciting hands-on science center near you or

find one on your next vacation.

HCC Dinosaurs

http://www.hcc.hawaii.edu/dinos/dinos.1.html
See and learn about a Triceratops Skull,
Tyrannosaurus rex head, Stegosaurus Skeleton and a
Baby Hypselosaurus sculpture.

Helping Your Child Learn Science

http://www.ed.gov/pubs/parents/Science/index.html
Discover ideas for projects and activities for in the
home and in the community.

The Human Heart

http://sln.fi.edu/biosci/heart.html
An online exploration of the human heart. Follow
the blood through the blood vessels and discover
the heart's structure.

Invention Dimension

http://web.mit.edu/invent/
Find out who is the Inventor of the Week and learn
about American inventors and their creations. The
site also features invention related links and
resources.

Junior Scientists of Planet Earth

http://www.tasmall.com.au/drmatrix/junior.htm
Explore the links and information on great inventors
and resources for students.

Kinetic City Super Crew

http://www.aaas.org/ehr/kcsuper.html/ehr/kcsuper.ht
ml

This is a science adventure show for kids with hands on science experiments. You will also find a list of radio stations that play their show.

The Learning Web

http://www.usgs.gov/education/index.html

Investigate topics about the Earth that affect people daily and find a collection of resources to teach earth science concepts.

Mathematics and Science Education

http://www.enc.org:80/index.htm

The Eisenhower National Clearinghouse site features an innovator of the month, math lesson plans and activities for the classroom.

Maya Adventure

http://www.sci.mus.mn.us/sln/ma/

Maya Adventure includes images from the Science Museum of Minnesota's anthropological collections and fantastic experiments developed by the Science Museum's education division.

MicroWorlds

http://www.lbl.gov/MicroWorlds/

MicroWorlds is the Berkeley Laboratory's interactive science magazine for students in grades 9 through

12. Students can find answers to questions such as what makes a good electrical conductor and much more. This site also includes teacher's guides.

The Natural History Museum, Los Angeles

http://www.lam.mus.ca.us

Find a host of educational programs such as classes for schools, youth and family programs, adult lectures, classes, travel programs, community outreach programs, artifacts and specimens for loan, research programs for high school students and volunteer opportunities. Visit one of their online exhibits, other museums in Los Angeles or just find out what the weather is like in Los Angeles.

NCSA Education Program

http://www.ncsa.uiuc.edu/Edu/EduHome.html

Through the programs and exhibits this site links scientific research and education.

Ontario Science Center

http://www.osc.on.ca/

Discover web connections, an interactive zone, job opportunities and a description, time and cost of all the educational programs and workshops they have to offer.

Oregon Museum of Science and Industry

http://www.omsi.edu/

> Why is the sky blue? What are clouds made of? If you have a question you would like OMSI to answer, go to "Science Whatzit?" to test their knowledge and improve yours.

Paleontology Without Walls

http://www.ucmp.berkeley.edu/exhibit/exhibits.html

> This is the University of California Museum of Paleontology's site that covers Phylogeny, geology and evolutionary thought. It includes an online catalog of their collection and other museums collection.

Science Fair Home page

http://www.stemnet.nf.ca/~jbarron/scifair.html

> Discover science project ideas from a beginner level for grades 1 through 4 to an advanced level of high school science plus cool links.

Sierra Club's Meager Mountain Slide Show

http://www.sierraclub.ca/bc/projects/meager/images

> Tranquil images of Meager Mountain.

Smithsonian Institution

http://www.si.edu

> Explore the categories of places, people, activities, perspectives, resources and products. Go to the list of events and activities to see a list of current exhibitions covering the arts, sciences and history.

Virtual Frog Dissection

http://teach.virginia.edu/go/frog/   or
http://curry.edschool.Virginia.EDU/go/frog/

Virtually dissect a frog through this on-line tutorial
and step-by-step you will learn the anatomy of a frog.

Volcano World

http://volcano.und.nodak.edu/

This award winning site has everything to know
about volcanoes and includes volcano images and
virtual field trips to places like Mars and Hawaii.

Wacky Patent

http://colitz.com/site/wacky.htm

Did you know Harry Houdini invented a diving suit?
Find out what the wacky patent of the month is at
this award winning site. You can also visit prior
wacky patents and inventor links.

You Can with Beakman and Jax

http://www.nbn.com:80/youcan/index.html

This award winning site has interactive demos,
tremendous places to go and children can submit
questions. It also links to the crazy science show,
Beakman's World.

SPACE

Astronomy and Space Science

http://info.er.usgs.gov/network/science/astronomy/index.html

> Explore a list of numerous links to sites relating to astronomy and space science. Go to the MIT-Millstone Hill Observatory to learn about the Young Scholars Summer Program for middle school students at
> http://hyperion.haystack.edu/homepage.html

Earth and Universe

http://www.eia.brad.ac.uk

> Take a tour of the stars and galaxies or use the telescope to examine the sky via the web. The site also features Weather System reports.

Earth Viewer

http://www.fourmilab.ch/earthview/vplanet.html

> View a global topographic map or view the earth from the Sun, the Moon or pick a location by specifying the longitude, latitude and altitude.

Liftoff

http://liftoff.msfc.nasa.gov/

> Visit the Mission Operations Laboratory and learn about future missions and find Liftoff's current "What's Cool" link.

Magellan Mission to Venus

http://www.jpl.nasa.gov/magellan/

Discover the photo gallery, questions, fact sheets, animation, the Magellan Venus Explorer's Guide and more. You can find more information on this mission at:

http://nssdc.gsfc.nasa.gov/planetary/magellan.html

The Messier Catalog

http://seds.lpl.arizona.edu/messier/Messier.html

Feast your eyes on 109 images of the best and brightest deep sky objects. Learn about nebulae, star clusters, galaxies and more.

NASA

http://www.nasa.gov/

Discover cool NASA web sites or read the latest news about NASA science and technology.

NASA Shuttle Web Archives

http://shuttle.nasa.gov/index.html/

Explore past, recent and future missions and the different stages of a mission.

NASA's Planetary Photojournal

http://photojournal.jpl.nasa.gov/

Hundreds of images of the planets in our solar system.

The Nine Planets

http://www.seds.org/billa/tnp/

Take a multimedia tour of the solar system.

Ocean Planet

http://seawifs.gsfc.nasa.gov/ocean_planet.html

This site is by the Smithsonian Institution's National Museum of Natural History and includes lessons plans and information on marine science activities.

Shuttle Launch Countdown Homepage

http://www.ksc.nasa.gov/shuttle/countdown/

Find information on space shuttle launches, a countdown, status, Today at NASA, photo archives and recent shuttle missions information including links to NASA Public Affairs, NASA Home Page, KSC Home Page and KSC Public Affairs Home.

Solar System

http://www.hawastsoc.org/solar/homepage.htm

Views and information about our solar system. See incredible images of the sun, moons, planets, asteroids, comets and meteoroids. The primary address for this site will be the Planetary Society.

Solar System Visualization Home Page

http://www-pdsimage.JPL.NASA.GOV/SSV/

View fantastic images and movies of outer space.

Space Shuttle Monitor

http://www.prairienet.org/~tgnally/shuttle.html
View live video, links to Nasa today and photos of current shuttle operations.

Space Telescope's Greatest Hits

http://www.stsci.edu/pubinfo/BestOfHST95.html
View incredible images in the photo gallery of the universe.

Space Views

http://www.seds.org/spaceviews/
This publication of the Boston Chapter of the National Space Society offers news, articles and book reviews for high school level and up.

The StarChild Project

http://heasarc.gsfc.nasa.gov/docs/StarChild/StarChild.html
This site is a learning center for young astronomers. Kids can discover information about the Moon, Planets, Asteroid Belt and much more in a user friendly and fun environment.

Star Maps

http://www.mtwilson.edu/Services/StarMap/
Enter the date, time and location of the star map you would like.

SPORTS

Basketball Tips for Kids

http://www.prostar.com/web/northshr/bb-tips.htm
This is a page of tips on the fundamentals of basketball for coaching children and adults.

ESPNET Sports Zone

http://espnet.sportszone.com/
Listen to live audio news on Baseball, NBA, NFL, NHL, Soccer, Tennis and other sports. This site requires a subscription.

Sports Illustrated for Kids

http://pathfinder.com/SIFK/
Children can find out the latest sports news, send in their works of art and ask questions.

Trips For Kids

http://www.webcom.com/tfk/
This non-profit volunteer organization in the San Francisco Bay Area provides mountain biking outings, environmental education and bicycle mechanics training for low income youth.

World Wide Web of Sports

http://www.tns.lcs.mit.edu/cgi-bin/sports/
Connections to pages on dozens of sports organizations like the NFL Page, Texas Rodeo Sports News,

Australian Soccer Homepage and the U.S.A. gymnastics online.

ALL SUBJECTS

Edison Odyssey of the Mind Creativity Site
http://mars.superlink.net/user/lsemel/om.html

http://www.odyssey.org/odyssey/

This non-profit organization "promotes creative team based problem solving in a school program for students from kindergarten through college". The projects can involve building spring driven vehicles to an interpretation of a literary classic.

Education Place
http://www.eduplace com/hmco/school/index.html

Features project ideas for social studies, reading/language arts, math, online projects, science, key pals and more.

Educational Links
http://www.onlinex.net/educate.html

Find lesson plans, project ideas and links to math, science, art, reading and literature.

PBS Online
http://www.pbs.org/

Discover a list of PBS series sites like The Magic

School Bus. Read news, articles and learn with PBS on the electronic field trips or PBS mathline.

Whales

http://curry.edschool.Virginia.EDU/~kpj5e/Whales/
This site has teacher resources, student activities, whale projects, internet resources, and categories in math, science, language arts, social studies, critical thinking and whale research.

The World Lecture Hall

http://www.utexas.edu/world/lecture/index.html
Choose a subject and find syllabi, assignments, lecture notes, exams, class calendars, textbooks and more.

WorldVillage

http://www.worldvillage.com/
The WorldVillage features software reviews, educational downloads and a section for kids. The village also offers games and early childhood activities.

Genius is one percent inspiration and ninety-nine per cent perspiration. —Thomas Alva Edison, Life

ORGANIZATIONS
PROVIDING
INFORMATION

ALLPIE

Post Office Box 59

East Chatman, New York 12060-0059

518-392-6900

http://www.croton.com/allpie/

> The Alliance for Parental Involvement in Education, ALLPIE, is a nonprofit organization designed to help parents who wish to be involved in their children's education. They publish a resource list of catalogs, newsletters, brochures and flyers concentrating on educational materials for children. The list covers topics such as math activities with everyday materials, italic handwriting, and foreign language tools. They also publish the newsletter Options In Learning as well as sponsor conferences and workshops.

American Academy of Orthopedic Surgeons

Post Office Box 1998

Des Plaines, Illinois 60017

800-824-BONES

> For a free Play It Safe brochure call the Academy's public service telephone number or send a self-addressed business size envelope to Play It Safe at the above address.

American Academy of Pediatrics

Department C - Toy Safety

141 Northwest Point Blvd.

Post Office Box 927

Elk Grove Village, Illinois 60009-0927

800-433-9016
Outside the U.S. & Canada 847-228-5005
http://www.aap.org
> They have brochures on numerous topics such as
> toy safety and a catalog of books and videos includ-
> ing titles such as Baby, Child and Adolescent Care,
> Sources of Lead Poisoning, Swimming Lessons and
> Bicycle Safety.

American Academy of Periodontology
Suite 800
737 N. Michigan Avenue
Chicago, Illinois 60611-2690
> Send a self-addressed stamped envelope to receive a
> free pamphlet on Caring For Your Child's Teeth and
> Gums.

American Society For Auto Safety
800-424-9393
> Call for information regarding auto and car seat safe-
> ty.

Consumer Information Center
Post Office Box 100
Pueblo, Colorado 81002
719-948-4000
http://www.pueblo.gsa.gov
> Ask for a free consumer information catalog which
> offers tips on children, food and money. The catalog
> lists over 200 publications from a variety of federal

agencies. Some examples of brochures they offer are Helping Your Child Learn Math and Books for Children.

Federal Trade Commission

Public Reference
Washington, D.C. 20580
202-326-2222
http://www.ftc.gov

> The Federal Trade Commission publishes brochures on products and services, health and fitness and more.

Free Loan Program

Gospel Films, Inc.
Post Office Box 455
Muskegon, Michigan 49443-0455
Fax 616-777-7598
http://www.freemedia.org

> This leading non-profit producer and distributor of free films for use in junior and senior high schools offers videos that focus on topics such as coaching, decision making, peer pressure, self-esteem, racial differences, intimacy, depression, religious faith and substance abuse.

National Association for the Education of Young Children

1509 16th Street, N.W.
Washington, DC 20036-1426

202-232-8777
800-424-2460
Fax 202-328-1846
http://www.naeyc.org/naeyc

> The mission of the NAEYC is to inform and gather together people interested in the education of children from birth to age eight to improve the education and well-being of young children and to improve professional standards and educational opportunities of teachers. The association is for students, instructors and parents. A few of their services include books, brochures and video tapes on parenting and teaching, conferences and programs. The National AEYC publishes a magazine six times a year from November through September called *Young Children*, the journal for early childhood educators. They also have an Early Childhood Resources Catalog. They have member resources and benefits. Call to find a local or state Affiliate Group closest to you.

National Endowment for the Humanities

Room 402
1100 Pennsylvania Avenue, N.W.
Washington, D.C. 20506
800-NEH-1121
202-606-8282 For The Hearing Impaired
http://www.neh.fed.us

> The NEH offers information on their programs such as seminars and grants for teachers and reading and writing programs for children. Ask for the Overview

of Endowment Programs or a list of Timeless Classics
for grades K through 12.

U.S. Consumer Safety Product Commission

Washington, DC 20207
800-638-2772
800-638-8270 For The Hearing Impaired
301-504-0580
http://www.cpsc.gov

> The CPSC gives you access to press releases, recall
> notices and publications such as the Product Safety
> Review. This site also has a wealth of information on
> product and toy safety.

U.S. Department of Education

Washington, DC 20202
800-872-5327
202-401-0113
http://www.ed.gov/pubs/parents.html

> Call to receive a free copies of publications from the
> U.S. Department of Education on topics such as
> learning to read, preparing your child for college and
> financial aid.

There is only one corner of the universe you can be certain of
improving, and that's your own self.
–Aldous Huxley, Time Must Have a Stop

INDEXES

Subject Index

Index of Resources and Subjects

To Order Copies of
Discover Educational Toys For Children
for your friends and family

Call 1-800-444-2524

or
send check to:
Scholar Books
P.O. Box 471048
San Francisco, CA 94147
$12.95 plus $2.50 for shipping

Name

Address

City

State/Zip

Total number of books   x $12.95=

Shipping $2.50 for the first book and   +

$1.00 for each additional book   =

Total amount enclosed

Notes